LIFE

Anne Frank

Her Life and Her Legacy

ANNE AT SCHOOL in the Netherlands in 1940.

CONTENTS

FRONT COVER A portrait of Anne Frank in May 1942, and a page from her diary, written in October of that year. PHOTOGRAPHS FROM ANNE FRANK FONDS, BASEL/GETTY

BACK COVER The swinging bookcase that hid the *Achterhuis*. PHOTOGRAPH BY PIERO OLIOSI/POLARIS

THE WESTERKERK church tower that Anne would gaze at from the annex.

GRANGER

LIFE

EDITORIAL DIRECTOR Kostya Kennedy
DIRECTOR OF PHOTOGRAPHY Christina Lieberman
ART DIRECTOR Mimi Park
EDITOR Lily Rothman
WRITER Daniel S. Levy
COPY CHIEF Parlan McGaw
COPY EDITOR Joel Van Liew
PICTURE EDITOR Rachel Hatch
WRITER-REPORTER Amy Lennard Goehner
PHOTO ASSISTANT Alessandra Bianco

TIME INC. BOOKS
PUBLISHER Margot Schupf
ASSOCIATE PUBLISHER Allison Devlin
VICE PRESIDENT, FINANCE Terri Lombardi
VICE PRESIDENT, MARKETING Jeremy Biloon
EXECUTIVE DIRECTOR, MARKETING SERVICES Carol Pittard
DIRECTOR, BRAND MARKETING Jean Kennedy
SALES DIRECTOR Christi Crowley
ASSISTANT GENERAL COUNSEL Andrew Goldberg
ASSISTANT DIRECTOR, PRODUCTION Susan Chodakiewicz
SENIOR MANAGER, CATEGORY MARKETING Bryan Christian
BRAND MANAGER Katherine Barnet
PREPRESS MANAGER Alex Voznesenskiy
ASSOCIATE PROJECT AND PRODUCTION MANAGER Anna Riego

EDITORIAL DIRECTOR Kostya Kennedy
CREATIVE DIRECTOR Gary Stewart
DIRECTOR OF PHOTOGRAPHY Christina Lieberman
EDITORIAL OPERATIONS DIRECTOR Jamie Roth Major
SENIOR EDITOR Alyssa Smith
ASSOCIATE ART DIRECTOR Allie Adams
ASSISTANT ART DIRECTOR Anne-Michelle Gallero
COPY CHIEF Rina Bander
ASSISTANT MANAGING EDITOR Gina Scauzillo
ASSISTANT EDITOR Courtney Mifsud

TIME INC. PREMEDIA
Richard K. Prue (Director), Richard Shaffer (Production), Keith Aurelio, Kevin Hart, Rosalie Khan, Patricia Koh, Marco Lau, Brian Mai, Rudi Papiri, Clara Renauro

SPECIAL THANKS Brad Beatson, Melissa Frankenberry, Kristina Jutzi, Simon Keeble, Seniqua Koger, Kate Roncinske, Kristen Zwicker

Published by LIFE Books, an imprint of Time Inc. Books, 225 Liberty Street, New York, NY 10281

Vol. 17, No. 9 • May 12, 2017

We welcome your comments and suggestions about LIFE Books. Please write to us at: LIFE Books, Attention: Book Editors, P.O. Box 62310, Tampa, FL 33662-2310

If you would like to order any of our hardcover Collector's Edition books, please call us at 800-327-6388, Monday through Friday, 7 a.m.–9 p.m. Central Time.

PRESIDENT BILL CLINTON in 2015 dedicates an Anne Frank exhibit at his presidential library in Little Rock, Arkansas—home to a sapling from the *Achterhuis* chestnut tree.

The Lessons of Her Life

BY PRESIDENT BILL CLINTON

On June 12, 1942, Anne Frank received a small diary for her 13th birthday. She and her family had been living in Amsterdam for nine years after fleeing their native Germany in 1933, when the Nazis gained power and began stripping Jews of their most basic rights. Although the Franks found stability for several years, they could not escape the wave of turmoil and repression sweeping across Europe. Less than a month after Anne received her diary, she and her family went into hiding to avoid being sent to the Nazi camps.

For the next two years, Anne confided her innermost thoughts to her diary. Her chronicles of daily life paint a picture of a bright girl—full of hopes and fears and love for her family and friends—navigating the passage from childhood into adulthood in a savagely cruel world that could not crush her heart, imagination, and dreams of the future. In one entry in 1944, she described her love of writing and her desire to make a career of it one day, saying, "I want to be useful or bring enjoyment to all people, even those I've never met. I want to go on living even after my death!"

She got her wish far too soon. Her diary comes to an abrupt end in August of 1944, when she and the others hiding in the "Secret Annex" at Prinsengracht 263 were discovered, arrested, and sent to concentration camps. Anne, her sister, Margot, and her mother, Edith, all died there. Her father, Otto, miraculously survived and upon returning to Amsterdam learned of Anne's diary. He dedicated the rest of his life to sharing her story with the world so that the same tragedy that befell his family and millions of others might never be repeated.

Now, 70 years since the first publication of her diary, Anne Frank endures as one of the great messengers of our common humanity. Through her courage, her hope, and her unshakable faith in the goodness of people—despite the grave injustices visited upon her and her family throughout her brief life—she continues to give a voice and a face to the six million Jews who lost their lives in the Holocaust. Her short life left a long legacy, touching and inspiring generation after generation of people she never met.

I will never forget visiting the Anne Frank House when I was just 23 and thinking that I had already been alive eight years longer than she had been allowed. Like millions of people who have been moved by Anne Frank's story, I have tried my best since then to live my life in a way that redeems the years she could not have. Today, the Clinton Presidential Center in Little Rock is honored to be home to a sapling propagated from the tall chestnut tree outside the Anne Frank House. Just as Anne Frank looked at that tree's branches from her hiding place and dreamed of a better life, I hope that our tree will remind all visitors to the center that we are duty bound to share the future and ensure that the atrocities of the past are never repeated.

In this deeply troubled time when so many people around the world are divided by religious, racial, and ethnic differences, the lessons of Anne Frank's life are more important than ever. We would all do well to remember the wisdom of a young girl who taught us that we are all diminished when any person suffers unfairly because of who he or she is—and that our differences make life more interesting, but our common humanity matters much more. ■

"But where there's hope, there's life. It fills us with fresh courage and makes us strong again."

ANNE FRANK, JUNE 6, 1944

GARETH PATTERSON/AP

A Happy Childhood, A Looming Threat

Growing Up in Germany and the Netherlands

"Later on neither I nor anyone else will be interested in the musings of a thirteen-year-old schoolgirl. Oh well, it doesn't matter. I feel like writing."

ANNE FRANK, JUNE 20, 1942

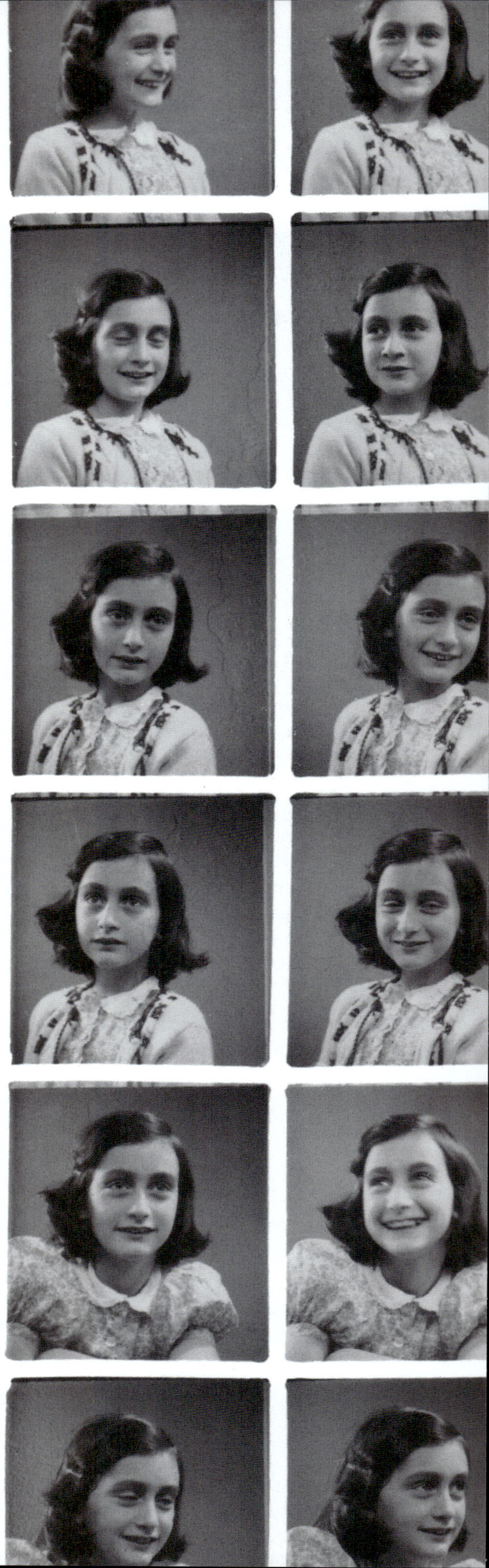

ANNE HAPPILY MUGGED for her passport photos in 1939, a year before the Nazis conquered the Netherlands and started their plans to round up Jews.

ANNE FRANK FONDS, BASEL/GETTY

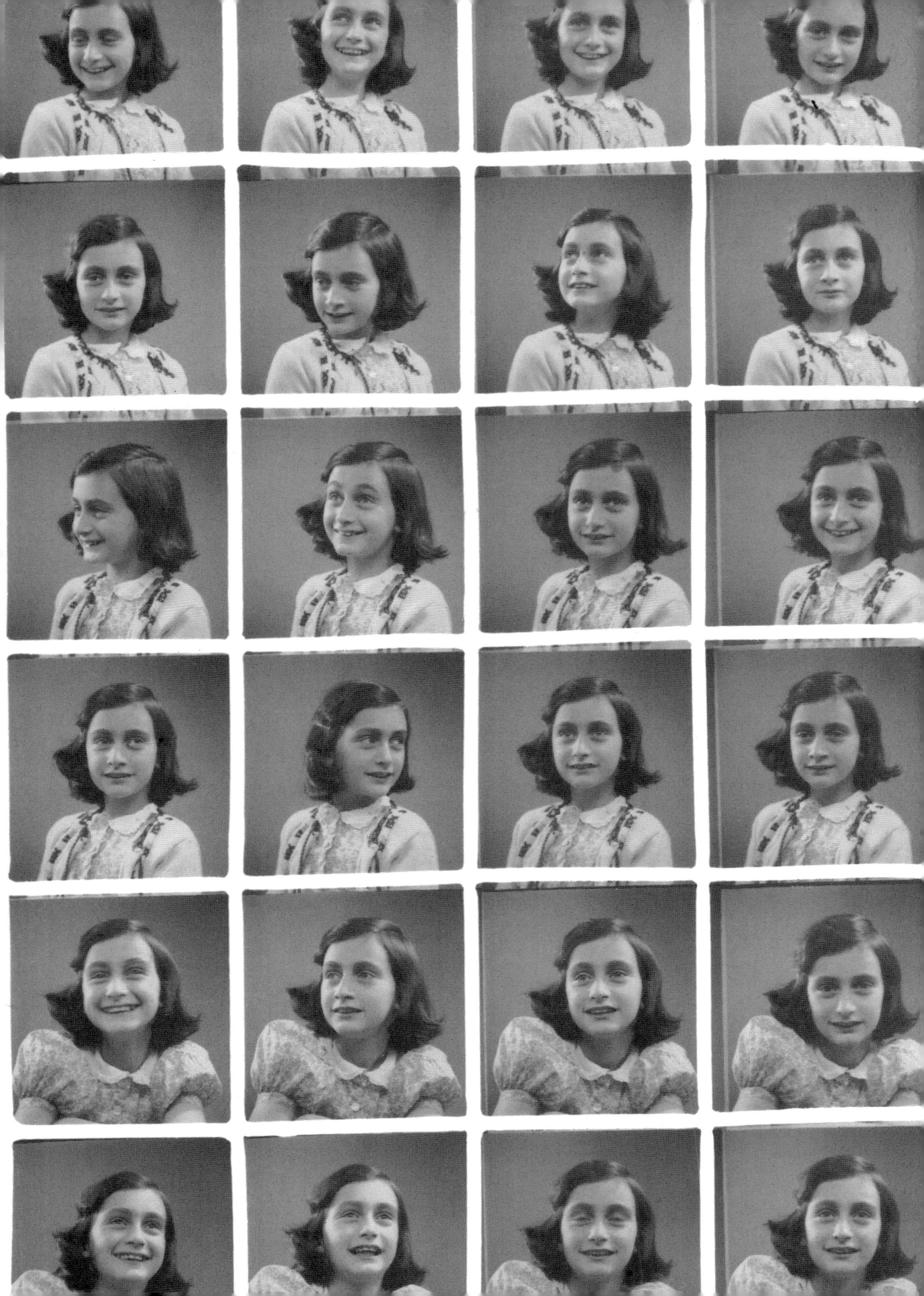

ANNE FRANK FONDS, BASEL/GETTY (3)

Things were good for the Frank family. Prosperous, cultured, and fervently patriotic, they had lived in Frankfurt for generations. During World War I, Otto Heinrich Frank had bravely served in the German army. After the war, he ran the family bank and the Soden Mineral Products Company, which made cough lozenges.

His entry into German business in the years following the war seemed to have come at a fortuitous time. The economy was improving after a period of hyperinflation. Not only was the improvement good for German wallets, it also helped to keep politics stable. Though National Socialism—the Nazi party—had raised its head in the early 1920s, the party received just 810,100 votes out of 31.2 million in the 1928 election for the Reichstag, the national parliament.

By then Otto was married to Edith Holländer, and they had started a family, settling in the Marbachweg section

CONTINUED ON PAGE 12

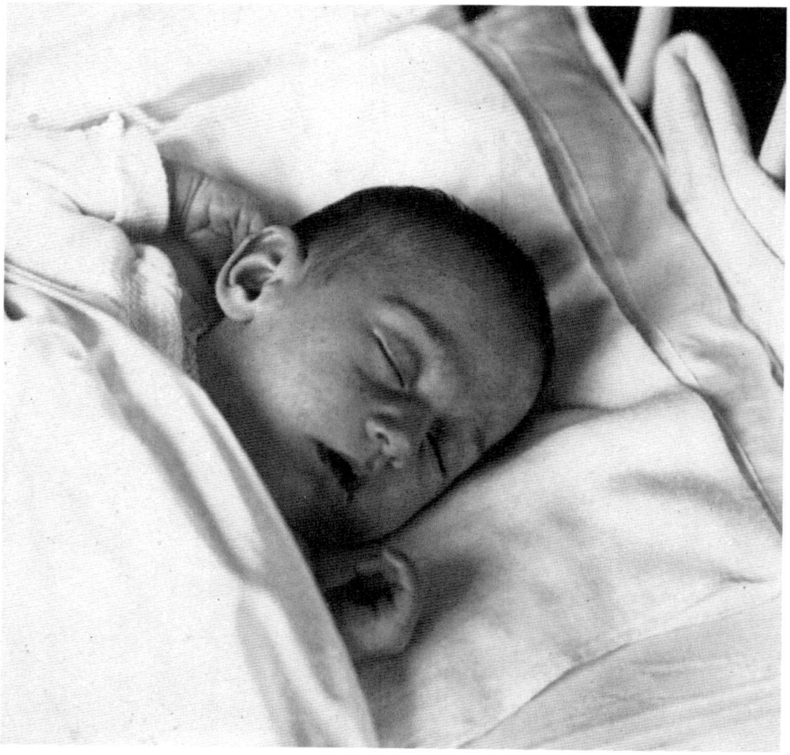

IN 1925, OTTO AND EDITH were married in Aachen, Germany, top. The couple honeymooned in San Remo, Italy. Above: An infant Anne asleep in Frankfurt. Opposite: Margot and Edith in a photo booth in July 1928.

A PORTRAIT of two-year-old Anne from May 1931 that she kept in her photo album. Opposite: Anne and Margot in 1933. Later that year, Otto set up his business in Amsterdam. Soon after, Edith and the girls would join him.

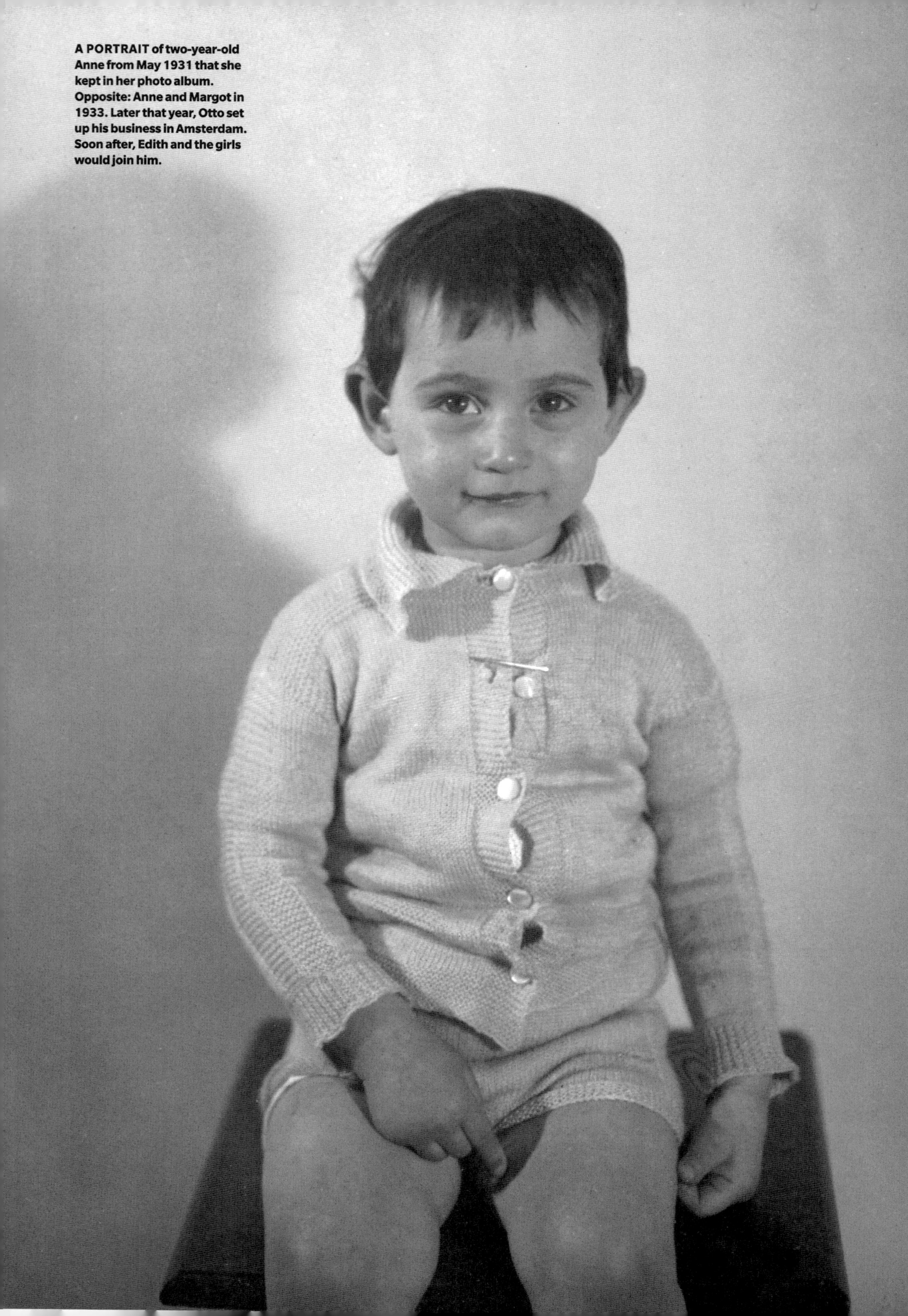

ANNE FRANK FONDS, BASEL/GETTY (2)

CONTINUED FROM PAGE 8

of town. Their eldest, Margot Betty, arrived in February 1926. Three years later, on June 12, 1929, she was followed by Annelies Marie.

While Margot was more demure, Anne, with huge green eyes and slight buckteeth, quickly developed into a charming and lively girl. Frankfurt had one of the largest Jewish populations in Germany. Jews and their Christian neighbors got along, and Edith would recall her life there as "among our best times." The Franks regularly entertained, with Edith serving meat stews, wurst, and other dishes. Unlike many fathers of that era, Otto, whom Anne called "the most adorable father I've ever seen," was an attentive and patient dad and husband who played with his children and served his wife breakfast in bed on Sundays.

But outside the family circle, the world was changing. Though the Nazi party had failed in the 1928 elections, its Austrian leader, Adolf Hitler, had produced an autobiography, *Mein Kampf,* and crisscrossed his adopted nation to warn of the dangers of communism and the demonic evils of

IMAGNO/GETTY

ANNE FRANK FONDS, BASEL/GETTY (2)

FRANKFURT WAS ONCE a vibrant Jewish center. The Friedberger Anlage synagogue, above, seated 1,600 congregants. Top right: The Frank family home in the city. Right: Anne, in white, with Edith and Margot in 1933 at Hauptwache, a central plaza in Frankfurt.

CENTRAL PRESS/GETTY

the Jewish people, whom he called "destroyers of culture." When the world economy plummeted in 1929, Hitler's fortunes soared. As the Great Depression battered the poor and the rich, worker and industrialist, Jew and Gentile, many Germans started to listen to his call for a strong and purified nation.

The crash battered the Franks. As the economy continued to decline, income from the lozenge company dried up and the family bank teetered. At the same time, more and more people adopted Nazism. After receiving just 2.6 percent of the vote in 1928, the Nazi party captured 18 percent in 1930. Otto commented on the political climate to a cousin, "I don't like it. I don't know what's going to happen. I'm scared of the right." In July 1932, the

FPG/HULTON/GETTY

IN 1933, GERMANS cheered President Paul von Hindenburg, above, after he voted in the November general elections. Ten months had already passed since he had appointed Adolf Hitler chancellor of Germany. By then Hitler had ruthlessly started consolidating power. At left, young Berliners giving the *Sieg Heil* salute. Opposite: Nazis raptly listened to Hitler after the party's March 1933 victory.

BETTMANN/GETTY

Nazis captured 37.3 percent of the vote.

The following January, Hitler became chancellor of Germany. The effect was immediate. The Nazis called for a boycott of Jewish businesses and banned Jews from government work, and Jewish children could only go to all-Jewish schools. Stunned, many Jews looked for ways to emigrate. One place they looked to was the Netherlands, where Jews made up 10 percent of the population of the capital, Amsterdam. Otto had worked in Holland 10 years earlier and knew the language.

Otto went to Amsterdam, and in September he registered the Dutch Opekta Joint-Stock Company business, a subsidiary of a German firm that made a jelling agent for jam. He and Edith found an apartment in Merwedeplein, a new housing development in the River Quarter. And, as the tide of Nazi power rose in Frankfurt, the Franks left.

Four-year-old Anne was thin as a wisp, curious, mercurial, and a know-it-all. She and Margot quickly adapted to their new home, becoming fluent in Dutch and eagerly taking to

BERLINER VERLAG/ARCHIV/PICTURE-ALLIANCE/DPA/AP

GRANGER

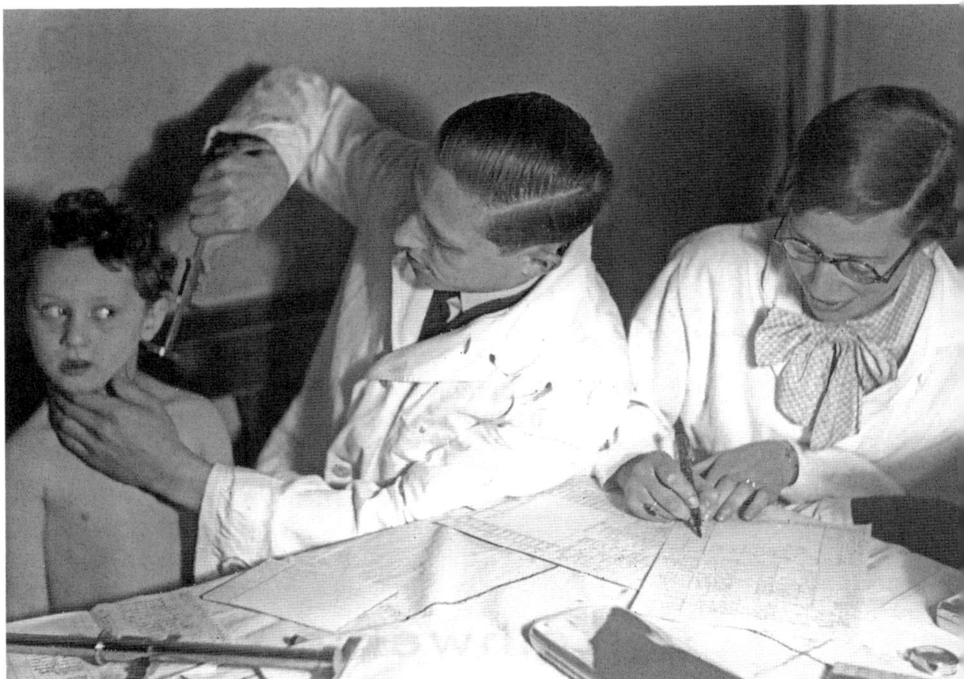

BILDARCHIV PISAREK/AKG-IMAGES

NAZIS BOYCOTTED Jewish businesses. Above: A man stood in front of a shop, with a sign reading "Germans! Defend yourselves! Don't buy from Jews!" Top right: Police harassed an elderly Jewish man. Right: A medical examination sought evidence of Jews' genetic inferiority.

IN 1934, ANNE enjoyed time on a beach in the Netherlands, above. She visited Switzerland to see relatives in 1935, left. Opposite: Anne, at right, posed with friends Eva Goldberg, left, and Susanne "Sanne" Ledermann in front of their Amsterdam apartment building in 1936. "All the kids came out to play on the big open triangle plaza," her friend Eva Schloss tells LIFE. "Skipping and hopscotch and marbles and talking."

ice-skating and biking. Shortly after the Franks met Ruth Goslar and her daughter Hannah, who had also just moved to town from Germany, Anne and Hannah started kindergarten together. "From then on she was a good friend," Hannah Pick-Goslar tells LIFE. "We did everything together."

Otto meanwhile built up Opekta and hired a congenial staff. Victor Kugler, who had served in the Austrian navy, helped run the firm. Amsterdammer Elisabeth "Bep" Voskuijl worked as a shorthand typist. Johannes "Jo" Kleiman, from Koog aan de Zaan, north of Amsterdam, kept the books. Otto "was always our boss but also our father," said Hermine "Miep" Santrouschitz, a

ANNE FRANK FONDS, BASEL/GETTY (3)

petite woman from Vienna, who did billing and office chores.

While the firm grew, Germany annexed Austria in March 1938, and Nazi ideology emboldened Dutch fascistic groups to vandalize Jewish property. Otto's employees urged him to move his family once again, to leave the business and go somewhere safer. He told them he would stay, Miep would later recall, because he loved the Netherlands. In October 1938, Hitler took the Sudetenland, a German-speaking section of Czechoslovakia, a nation that bordered Germany to the east. The following month, Gestapo chief Heinrich Müller instigated *Kristallnacht*—the Night of Broken Glass—during which German citizens burned hundreds of synagogues and looted thousands of shops. In March, Hitler's forces entered the Czech capital, Prague.

By then, Otto ran both Opekta and Pectacon, a firm that produced chemical products and foodstuffs. To help with the added work, he hired Hermann van Pels, a Jewish butcher who along with his wife, Auguste, and son, Peter, had arrived in Amsterdam from Germany in July of 1937. Eventually Jews made up a third of the 50,000 residents of the River Quarter. The Franks were very social, regularly hosting coffee on weekends for visitors like the van Pels family

CONTINUED ON PAGE 24

ANNE FRANK FONDS, BASEL/GETTY (2)

ANNE IN MRS. BALDAL'S class at a Montessori school in Amsterdam, above, seated between two desks in the corner near the door. Margot posed for a student picture at the Jeker School in Amsterdam in 1936, right.

HUGO JAEGER/THE PICTURE COLLECTION, INC.

IN 1938, ELITE SS units—participation in which was considered an honor among Nazis—marked the swearing-in of new members with an elaborate ceremony in Munich. During the ritual they pledged to Hitler absolute allegiance until death.

CONTINUED FROM PAGE 20

and dentist Fritz Pfeffer, who had fled Germany after Kristallnacht, as well as Miep and her fiancé, Jan Gies.

"Edith was a good German housewife," Anne's friend Eva Schloss tells LIFE. "She made lemonade and cookies and biscuits. There always was some snack."

And yet, eventually Otto Frank's love of the Netherlands was not enough. In September 1939, Germany invaded Poland and Otto frantically searched for ways to get his family away from the growing conflict. He hoped to emigrate to the United States, though he turned down an offer from a cousin to care for the girls in England, because he didn't want to separate the family.

Then on May 10, 1940, everyone's fears came true.

Germany launched what it called *Fall Gelb,* an attack on the Netherlands, France, Belgium, and Luxembourg. On the 13th, Dutch queen Wilhelmina and her cabinet fled, asking her subjects to "think of our Jewish compatriots." The next day, German bombers set off a firestorm in Rotterdam that killed nearly 900 people and destroyed more than 27,000 buildings. The Dutch commander in chief, General Henri G. Winkelman, had no choice but to surrender.

Some 140,000 Jews lived in the Netherlands, and the geography made

FINE ART IMAGES/HERITAGE IMAGES/GETTY

"Where they burn books, they will also ultimately burn people."

POET HEINRICH HEINE, 1821

GRANGER

DURING *KRISTALLNACHT*, the Night of Broken Glass, in November 1938, Germans rampaged against Jewish businesses and homes. Nazi propaganda minister Joseph Goebbels saw it as a chance to "rise in bloody vengeance against the Jews." In Mosbach, above, left, they burned the furnishings and ritual objects from the town synagogue. In the town of Ober-Ramstadt, right, firefighters allowed a synagogue to burn, ensuring only that the flames didn't spread to nearby homes. The government blamed the Jews themselves for Kristallnacht and fined them a total of $400 million. Jews filed insurance claims, but the government confiscated all monies from those claims.

"Submit to me as soon as possible a general plan of the administrative, material, and financial measures necessary for carrying out the desired final solution of the Jewish question."

HERMANN GÖRING, JULY 31, 1941

UNIVERSAL HISTORY ARCHIVE/UIG/GETTY

ULLSTEIN BILD/PRESSEFOTO KINDERMANN/AKG-IMAGES

IN SEPTEMBER 1939, in a blitzkrieg—"lightning war"—Germany invaded and captured Poland, above, in just a few weeks. *Einsatzgruppen*, mobile killing units made up of SS troops and police officers, moved through the land slaughtering Polish nationals and elites, and started their consolidation of Jews. In the spring of 1940 they established the Auschwitz concentration camp. Above, right: In Bydgoszcz, Poland, in 1939, civilians were killed in the street by firing squad.

it difficult to flee. Reichskommissar Arthur Seyss-Inquart ran the new civil administration and, at the start, many hoped that the occupying forces would not undermine day-to-day life. "When the Germans came in May 1940, they seemed to be proper men," recalled Joop Zoutberg, a non-Jew whose father worked in Amsterdam's matzo factory. "They did no harm that first time."

But repressions quickly began under SS general Hanns Rauter, who headed national security. Regulations barred Jews from civil service jobs, forced them to disclose their business assets, and segregated Jewish children to all-Jewish schools. "Jews Prohibited" appeared on signs in parks and cafés. Schloss bristled at the restrictions: "At first it was a nuisance; we couldn't go to the swimming pool or public transport or the cinema." The movie rule especially bothered the cinema-obsessed Anne, so Otto rented movies and a projector to show films at home.

Then, in January 1941, the Germans required Jews to register in order to compile a record of the country's 159,806 Jews and 19,561 mixed Jews. "This was a system of self-reporting. So anybody with Jewish grandparents had to report that to the authorities," Gertjan Broek, a historian at the Anne Frank House in Amsterdam

CONTINUED ON PAGE 30

ANNE FRANK FONDS, BASEL/GETTY

IN JUNE 1939, Anne (second from left) celebrated her 10th birthday, posing with friends outside her apartment. She had a large set of friends. Three years later, she would boast to her diary, "There are about 30 people I can call friends. I have a throng of admirers who can't keep their adoring eyes off of me."

ULLSTEIN BILD/GRANGER

BETTMANN/GETTY

CONTINUED FROM PAGE 27

tells LIFE. "Strange as it seems today, most people just did that."

Some joined the resistance, stealing ID cards and working with the Allies to sabotage bridges. And, after Germans assaulted Jews in the central square in February 1941, the Communist party called for a massive work stoppage. The action, instead of weakening the resolve of the Nazis, only inspired more repression. General Rauter crushed the strike, killing seven and wounding 76; 427 were apprehended and sent to the Buchenwald concentration camp.

Throughout, Otto's business grew. Needing more space, Opekta moved in December 1940 to a new address: Prinsengracht 263, an early-18th-century canal building near the famed 17th-century Westerkerk church. The narrow brick structure had four stories and was actually made up of two buildings, one of which was an annex in the back. Because of the growing restrictions on Jewish life, Otto quietly transferred control of his business to Jo Kleiman and Victor Kugler.

By now, the Nazis had explicitly laid out their plan to exterminate European Jewry. And, in early 1942, with the United States having entered the war in the wake of the Japanese attack on Pearl Harbor, the Nazis cracked down even more. They issued 569,355 yellow stars marked *Jood* and required Jews to sew them onto their clothes. "My brother, Heinz, told me that a friend of his who took off his star got arrested and he was never seen again," says Schloss.

With escape from Holland beginning to seem impossible, Otto Frank came up with a different idea.

He began, with the help of Kleiman and Kugler, to hatch a plan to hide

CONTINUED ON PAGE 34

IN MAY OF 1940, as German troops rolled into Amsterdam, non-Jewish German-speaking Dutch citizens greeted them, above. The famous Dutch bicycle regiment, opposite top, and the nation's other forces proved no match against the onslaught. German troops moved in, bottom, soon after the air force incinerated part of Rotterdam.

HUGO JAEGER/THE PICTURE COLLECTION, INC.

GAMMA-KEYSTONE/GETTY

ULLSTEIN BILD/GETTY

EDDIE WORTH/AP

TO AVOID CAPTURE and being used by the Nazis, Queen Wilhelmina, top, fled to England. Arthur Seyss-Inquart, above, who helped bring about the takeover of Austria, was made *Reichskommissar* of the Netherlands. Opposite: These children were among the few who escaped to England.

CONTINUED FROM PAGE 30

his family in Amsterdam. As a child, Miep had been a refugee, having been sent by her parents from Vienna to Amsterdam following World War I, when there was little food to be had in Austria. So when Otto asked her and Jan, whom she had just married, whether they were willing to take responsibility for a family in hiding, they unhesitatingly said yes. Bep Voskuijl soon became part of the group of helpers, and Otto invited Hermann van Pels and his family to join them in hiding. They created a small apartment in the back building at 263, behind the office. To prepare the place, they surreptitiously stocked it with canned goods, dried fish, grains, and other necessities, as well as furniture, bedding, kitchen utensils, and dishes.

Anne turned 13 in 1942, and for her June birthday party, Otto rented *The Lighthouse by the Sea,* starring Rin Tin Tin. Anne had recently admired a red plaid diary at a bookshop around the corner from their home and was thrilled to receive it as a gift. She called the book "one of my nicest presents," making her first entry that day, writing, "I hope I will be able to confide everything to you as I have never been able to confide to anyone. And I hope you will be a great source of comfort and support."

Anne treated her entries like

FOTOTECA GILARDI/AKG-IMAGES

"Fine specimens of humanity, those Germans . . . there are no greater enemies on earth than the Germans and the Jews."

ANNE FRANK, OCTOBER 9, 1942

ULLSTEIN BILD/GETTY

AS PART OF THE PLAN to round up Dutch Jews, the Germans gathered them at a central area, left, and sent them off to the camps. Most were sent to Westerbork, in northeast Netherlands, right. Under commandant Erich Deppner, trains punctually departed from there every Tuesday for the concentration camps. When Canadian troops liberated Westerbork in April 1945, they found only 876 inmates alive.

ANNE FRANK FONDS, BASEL/GETTY (2)

letters, eventually settling on an imaginary correspondent named Kitty, named for a character from a series of stories by Cissy van Marxveldt about a fun and carefree teenage girl with a best friend named Kitty. Despite what was going on around her, Anne stayed positive, heading with friends to Café Delphi or a local ice cream parlor, playing table tennis, and filling the diary's early pages with teenage thoughts about her crushes and friends.

On July 5, however, a letter arrived from the authorities for Margot.

Plans had been announced to send Jews age 16 to 40 to Germany for labor, and Margot was now being ordered to report. That night Jan and Miep picked up some clothes, towels, and shoes. The girls packed their schoolbags—"the first thing I stuck in was this diary, and then curlers, handkerchiefs, schoolbooks, a comb, and some old letters," wrote Anne. Otto sent a coded letter to his sister, Helene Elias, in Basel, Switzerland, to let her know that they were going to vanish.

"We knew then that they were going to hide," her son, Bernhard, would later say. "But we had no idea where. And from then on, there was no contact anymore." ■

MARGOT ENJOYED tennis and is seen wearing sunglasses, standing, second from left, with her teammates, above. She also rowed, and her team won a medal in 1940. When Jews were banned from the rowing club, her Christian teammates, in solidarity, refused to take part in races. Officials also denied Jews entry to Dutch schools, and Anne and Margot attended the Jewish Lyceum, where Anne—who had a reputation for her humor and for being a chatterbox—was photographed in 1941, opposite.

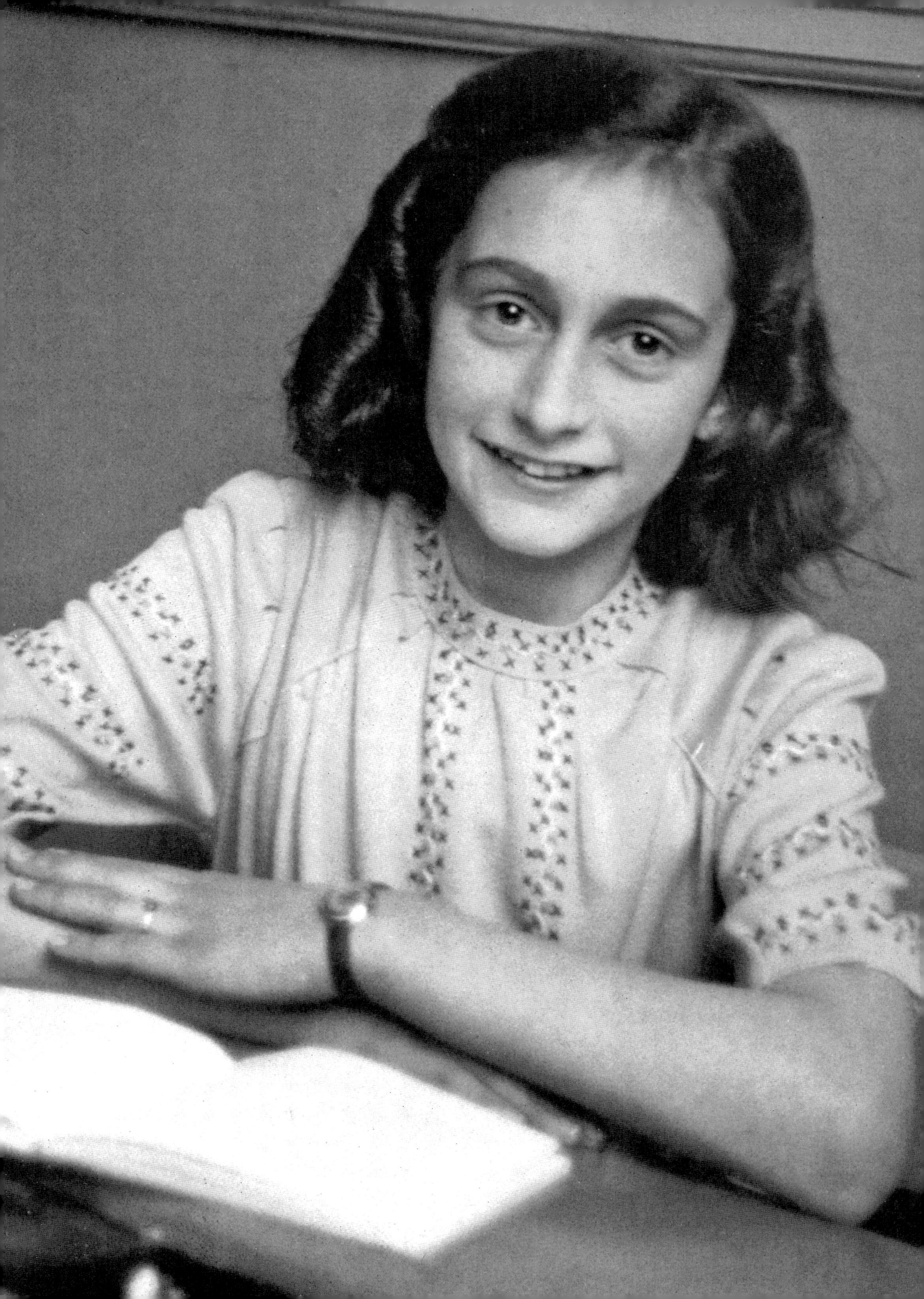

The Young Writer in Hiding

Twenty-five Months in the Secret Annex

"Whatever we do, we're very afraid the neighbors might hear or see us."

ANNE FRANK, JULY 11, 1942

THE DIARY, which became Anne's regular companion while in hiding, was a place for her to share her thoughts, frustrations, hopes, and fears, as well as photos from a happier time.

ADE JOHNSON/EPA/REDUX

denk ik nog
vaak en ik woon
dat hij nog wede
Margot en
ik kwamen
uit het wa-
ter en ik
weet nog ik
had het erg
koud, daar-
om heb ik mijn
badjas om-
gedaan
Margot en
ik
20 Sept. 1942

Achterhuis Residents

THE FRANK FAMILY
Otto, FATHER
Edith, MOTHER
Margot, DAUGHTER
Anne, DAUGHTER

THE VAN PELS FAMILY
Hermann, FATHER
Auguste, MOTHER
Peter, SON

Fritz Pfeffer, A DENTIST

Their Helpers

Miep Gies, OPEKTA EMPLOYEE
Jan Gies, MIEP'S HUSBAND
Bep Voskuijl, OPEKTA EMPLOYEE
Johan Voskuijl, OPEKTA WAREHOUSE MANAGER
Jo Kleiman, OPEKTA ACCOUNTANT
Victor Kugler, OPEKTA EMPLOYEE

ANNE FRANK FONDS, BASEL/GETTY

CSU ARCHIVES/EVERETT

AT THE BACK of the Opekta office and warehouse, left, was the *Achterhuis*, where the Frank and van Pels families and Fritz Pfeffer hid. Otto, above center, was a beloved boss. His employees—clockwise from left: Miep Gies, Jo Kleiman, Victor Kugler, and Bep Voskuijl—risked their lives to protect him and the others.

After Miep Gies arrived at the Frank home on the morning of July 6, 1942, she and Margot biked to Prinsengracht 263. Soon after, Anne, Otto, and Edith, wearing layers of clothes, walked the two and a half miles there. It was raining, and each carried a schoolbag and a shopping bag stuffed with as many items as could possibly fit. A week after the Franks settled in their hiding place, Hermann, Auguste, and Peter van Pels moved in. That November, Fritz Pfeffer would join them.

Even though the Franks had quietly spread the rumor that they planned to flee, many of their friends were still surprised to learn that they had vanished. "I came together with Jacqueline van Maarsen," Hannah Pick-Goslar tells LIFE. "We wanted to play with Anne. We rang the bell and nobody came to open. And after the third bell, the tenant who lived under the roof asked, 'What do you want?' He let us in. We heard from him that the Franks went to Switzerland."

As for what really happened to Anne and her family, her diary would prove to be the document that would tell the world the truth. That book became the teenager's constant companion, confidante, and friend. In it she detailed the day-to-day life of

ANNE FRANK FONDS, BASEL/GETTY (2)

"We're never far from Miep's thoughts."

ANNE FRANK, MAY 8, 1944

what she called the *Achterhuis,* literally the "back house," known in English as the Secret Annex.

That secret home was reached through Opekta's archives, accessed by way of a movable bookcase that Bep's father, Johan Voskuijl, had set on hinges. This entrance opened onto a small 540-square-foot living space. "No one would ever suspect there were so many rooms behind that plain gray door," Anne wrote. On the first floor, the Frank family had a living room–bedroom where Otto, Edith, and Margo slept. Next to it stood a narrow room shared by Anne and Fritz. Anne slept on a small divan with a few chairs to make it longer. She decorated the walls with pictures of the Dutch royal family, England's Queen Elizabeth, movie stars like Ginger Rogers and Greta Garbo, and artwork.

On the second floor, the van Pels couple stayed in the annex's largest room. It had been used as a lab, and contained a sink and a stove, so it doubled as a communal living room and kitchen where they all shared meals. Next to it was Peter's room, which was really just a landing with a ladder coming down from the attic. Peter, who was two and a half years older than Anne and who she initially found to be "a shy, awkward boy whose

MIEP JOINED the new firm of Opekta in 1933, and is seen there in 1936, above, left. Miep and Jan Gies married on July 16, 1941, opposite, and he helped to provide for those in hiding through his work with the Dutch resistance.

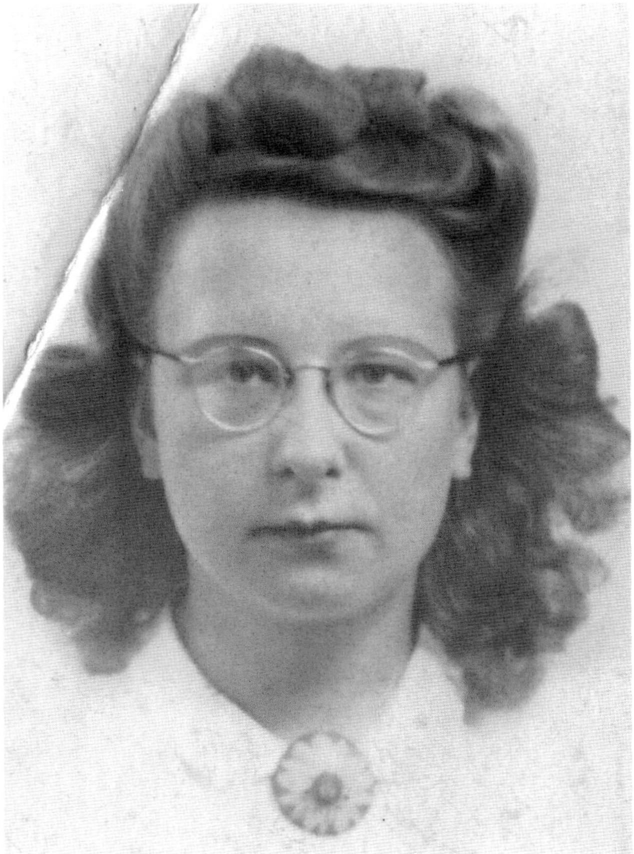

PHOTO COLLECTION ANNE FRANK HOUSE, AMSTERDAM (2)

GRANGER

THE ENTRANCE to the Achterhuis, opposite. Above, two of the protectors. At left, warehouse foreman Johan Voskuijl, who built the secret doorway, and of whom Anne said, "He's been most helpful." At right, his daughter, Bep, whom Anne described as "good-humored, kind, and willing."

company won't amount to much," decorated his space with photos of movie stars that Anne gave him. In the attic above, they stored food and supplies.

The residents arrived just in time. In July the Nazis began sending Dutch Jews to the Westerbork transit camp and from there to their deaths in Auschwitz and Sobibor. The Franks weren't the only ones refusing to surrender. In 1942 and 1943, some 25,000 Dutch Jews went into hiding, helped by neighbors, the Dutch underground, and strangers. Miep and Jan Gies even helped others beyond those in the Achterhuis; they briefly hid in their apartment Kuno van der Horst, a student who opposed the Nazis. "What happened to helpers could differ from nothing at all to being shot," Gertjan Broek at the Anne Frank House tells LIFE. "Being incarcerated was not very uncommon."

For example, while hiding, Eva Schloss's family had to keep moving to stay ahead of the authorities. "We had hiding places within the hiding places," she tells LIFE. "People were scared. At night the Nazis came and they searched the homes. You tried to sleep, but we were very alert."

The Franks' situation, though, was unusual. "I know of people who moved around, a few weeks here, a few weeks there," says Broek. "Some people were at 30 addresses. Being two intact families and one lodger, with children and parents not splitting up and staying at one place, was not a very common thing."

The Achterhuis building was filled during the day with Opekta workers, and the secret residents had tense and regimented days. They woke around 6:45 a.m. They took down the blackout curtains, washed, and got ready before 8:30, when the firm's workers arrived. While Johan Voskuijl knew they were there, most did not, and the eight in hiding had to tiptoe around in what Miep sensed was a fear "so thick I could feel it pressing down on me."

They ate breakfast in the van Pelses' room. In the morning, Anne, Margot, and Peter did their schoolwork. "Above all, the children had

to have enough books to read and learn," Otto would later recall. Anne kept busy with her diary too, pasting photos in its pages and writing about what she was studying ("shorthand in French, English, German, and Dutch, geometry, algebra, history, geography, art history, mythology, biology, Bible history, Dutch literature"), the books she liked best ("biographies, dull or exciting, and history books [sometimes novels and light reading]"), and what her compatriots and family were working on (English for Otto and Edith, trigonometry for Margot, and a variety of languages—plus woodworking—for Peter).

They had much time to pass, and everyone had to do what Anne called a "time killer." They endlessly discussed the war and prepared their own food, shelling pounds of peas, processing bratwurst and mettwurst, and having marathon canning sessions. Anne practiced ballet, tried different hairstyles, and shared her thoughts and experiences with her diary. "Oh, I am so glad I brought you along!" she wrote in September. "Kitty's always patient."

Each day, when Opekta's workers headed home for lunch, the residents relaxed a bit. They had lunch, and Bep, Jan, and Jo Kleiman might join them. After the staff left for the evening, the residents came downstairs. This Anne called their "nightly freedom." They had dinner and listened to the BBC and Radio Oranje. By 10 o'clock everyone was in bed, but with air raid sirens and Allied bombings, sleep often proved elusive. Sometimes machine-gun fire caused

"The reason I offered my help in looking after Otto Frank and his family during the time they were in hiding was because I had come to know him as a very decent and helpful person, qualities for which he is held in the highest esteem."

JO KLEIMAN

VICTOR KUGLER, opposite, came up with the idea to hide the entrance. "Mr. Kugler thought it would be better to have a bookcase built in front of the entrance to our hiding place," Anne wrote. "It swings out on its hinges and opens like a door." Jo Kleiman, right, worked hard to help those in the hiding place, despite suffering from a debilitating stomach ulcer.

ANNE FRANK FONDS, BASEL/GETTY (2)

ANNE FRANK FONDS, BASEL/GETTY

Anne to go into her parents' room to be comforted by her father. "I know it sounds childish," she wrote, "but wait till it happens to you!"

They couldn't open the windows in the summer, and it was cold in the winter. Yet Anne knew that they were lucky to be there. "I feel wicked sleeping in a warm bed, while somewhere out there my dearest friends are dropping from exhaustion or being knocked to the ground," she wrote. They all tried to find happiness, celebrating one another's birthdays, as well as Hanukkah and St. Nicholas Day, and making cookies, cakes, and other treats. They played board games like Monopoly and listened to music on the radio when they could.

But the claustrophobic environment led to heated arguments. During her visits, Miep could sense the tension, which she called "the sparks of unfinished conflicts left sizzling in the air." Anne wrote that "no matter what we say, someone is bound to resent it or take it the wrong way." This was especially true of Hermann and

ANNE AND PETER in 1942, just before they would go into hiding. In February 1944, Anne noticed that Peter had taken an interest in her, and he confided that he hoped to move to the Dutch East Indies after the war and live on a rubber plantation.

PHOTO COLLECTION ANNE FRANK HOUSE, AMSTERDAM

> *"I couldn't begin to imagine what they must be feeling to have walked away from everything they owned in the world—their home; a lifetime of gathered possessions; Anne's little cat, Moortje."*
>
> MIEP GIES IN HER MEMOIR, *ANNE FRANK REMEMBERED*

Auguste, whose fights often sprang from "something so trivial it didn't seem worth wasting a single word on."

Anne was a sensitive and impatient teenager. She felt that the other residents criticized her for everything, writing to Kitty, "my behavior, my personality, my manners; every inch of me, from head to toe and back again, is the subject of gossip and debate." While she adored Otto ("I model myself after father"), she had regular disagreements with Edith, who, she complained, babied her and bemoaned the fact that Anne wasn't more like her sister.

Anne harbored special disdain for the elder van Pelses, particularly Auguste, a "silly, sniveling specimen of humanity." She also disliked having to share a room with Pfeffer. As a growing teen, she felt uncomfortable with the invasion of her privacy, and found Pfeffer, whom she called Dussel (Dope) in her diary, to be a selfish, stodgy, "old-fashioned disciplinarian" who made "the sound of a fish gasping for air" when he slept.

Disagreements became more serious as the war progressed. With food becoming scarce, the residents quibbled over the division of what they had to eat. Pfeffer would "stuff himself behind our backs and not give us anything," Anne wrote, and the van Pels family was accused of "holding back meat and other things." As the months passed, some of their stock spoiled. Meanwhile, the Nazis caught some of those who had been supplying them with goods and coupons, which made it harder for the helpers to restock the pantry in the annex. The residents would have to subsist for days on end

THE FRANKS on a family outing in 1941, opposite. Above: Hermann and Auguste van Pels. The van Pelses left Germany in 1937, and Hermann started working for Otto in 1938. They moved into the Achterhuis a week after the Franks.

ANNE FRANK FONDS, BASEL/GETTY (3)

ANNE FRANK FONDS, BASEL/GETTY

on such meals as "endive with sand, endive without sand, endive with mashed potatoes, endive-and-mashed potato casserole."

Even with such hardship, those in the annex knew they were fortunate and were grateful for their protectors, who unstintingly brought them supplies and gifts. "Never have they uttered a single word about the burden we must be," Anne wrote.

Miep was their main benefactor. Anne adored her, for she always found time to talk to the residents, chatting with Anne about news, the movies, and fashion, and helping to console Edith. Each day Miep set out with a list of what they needed, pedaling her bicycle around town collecting supplies, causing Anne to write that "she looks like a pack mule." Bep helped too, and they searched the black market using forged ration books, getting meat from a friendly butcher, bread without ration tickets from a baker named Simons, and potatoes from greengrocer Hendrik van Hoeve. Jan Gies, who was active in a group that assisted those in hiding, would get false ration cards. Jo Kleiman and Victor Kugler also acquired ration coupons on the black market, and they would bring by much-appreciated newspapers and magazines.

Those small links to the outside world, while greatly desired, also underscored the seemingly endless confinement that made Anne crave "to breathe fresh air again . . . to ride a bike, dance, whistle, look at the world, feel young, and know that I'm free." Often she peeked through a space in the curtains, watching people walk and bicycle by or following what the family on a nearby houseboat was up to. She also retreated to the attic to write and gaze at the towering horse chestnut tree in the courtyard, as she listened to 51-bell carillon in the Westerkerk steeple, which "sounds so reassuring, especially at night." These were Anne's moments of peace. "As long as this exists," she wrote, "this sunshine and this cloudless sky, and as long as I can enjoy it, how can I be sad?"

Throughout it all, Anne wrote, letting Kitty know that she was "grateful to God" for having such a gift. In addition to her diary, she also wrote

CONTINUED ON PAGE 57

FRITZ PFEFFER, the eighth resident of the Achterhuis, above, with his son, Werner, at a Berlin lake in 1932. Fritz was able to save his son by getting him on a children's transport to England. Germany's Nuremberg race laws prevented Pfeffer from marrying his Christian girlfriend, Charlotte, seen with him in 1940, opposite. They escaped Germany after Kristallnacht and moved to Amsterdam.

PHOTO COLLECTION ANNE FRANK HOUSE, AMSTERDAM

"Our chestnut tree is in full bloom. It's covered with leaves and is even more beautiful than last year."

Anne Frank, May 13, 1944

PETER DEJONG/AP

ANNE AND PETER would escape to the attic and sit for hours discussing their hopes and plans for when they were finally free.

"The Jews for us are not Dutchmen. They are those enemies with whom we can come neither to an armistice nor to a peace."

ARTHUR SEYSS-INQUART, REICHSKOMMISSAR OF THE NETHERLANDS, MARCH 12, 1941

CONTINUED FROM PAGE 52

in notebooks. Soon, she started creating stories like "Eva's Dream," "The Secret Annex," and "Blurry the Explorer." As she wrote, her style matured to a level not often seen in a young teenager.

Soon, Anne started to revise her writing. This was a response to a March 1944 radio address by exiled Dutch education and culture minister Gerrit Bolkestein, who said that citizens needed to write about what they were enduring so that a "picture of Holland's struggle for freedom [could] be painted in its full depth and full glory." Anne dreamed of becoming a journalist and a writer, saying that "after the war I'd like to publish a book called *The Secret Annex*... My diary can serve as the basis."

As she honed her writing, she became a sharp and at times unforgiving observer of herself and those around her, musing on her developing sexuality and wondering when she would get her period and first kiss. She was happy that she and Margot were growing closer—her sister also kept a diary, and they occasionally read their entries to each other—and "longed unconsciously, and at times consciously, for trust, love, and physical affection."

As the months passed, moments of hope and the constant undercurrent of fear battled for space in the pages of Anne's diary.

She found herself unexpectedly attracted to Peter, finding beauty in his "dark blue eyes." The two would sit for long periods in the attic, talk about themselves, friends, and what they would do after the war, as well as about romance and sex. Anne longed "to fall in love with him." They kissed the first time in the spring of 1944, a moment that made her "too happy for words." Two weeks later, she let Kitty know that "we pressed our lips together. In a daze, we embraced, over and over again, never to stop, oh!... Now we've found each other."

And for a brief time, it seemed that Anne's burgeoning love might be a sign of even better things to come. As the summer of 1944 approached, radio broadcasts discussed the long-anticipated Allied invasion. When the residents finally heard of D-day and the start of the liberation of Europe, they excitedly hugged and wept, and Anne

FOTOTECA GILARDI/AKG-IMAGES

ULLSTEIN BILD/GRANGER

A JEWISH FAMILY in Amsterdam, opposite, reporting to an embarkation point, where they would be sent to a transit camp and then on to a concentration camp. Some 25,000 to 30,000 Jews, like those above, hid from the Nazis. Most were not as well prepared and cared for as the Franks, and many had to move numerous times to avoid capture.

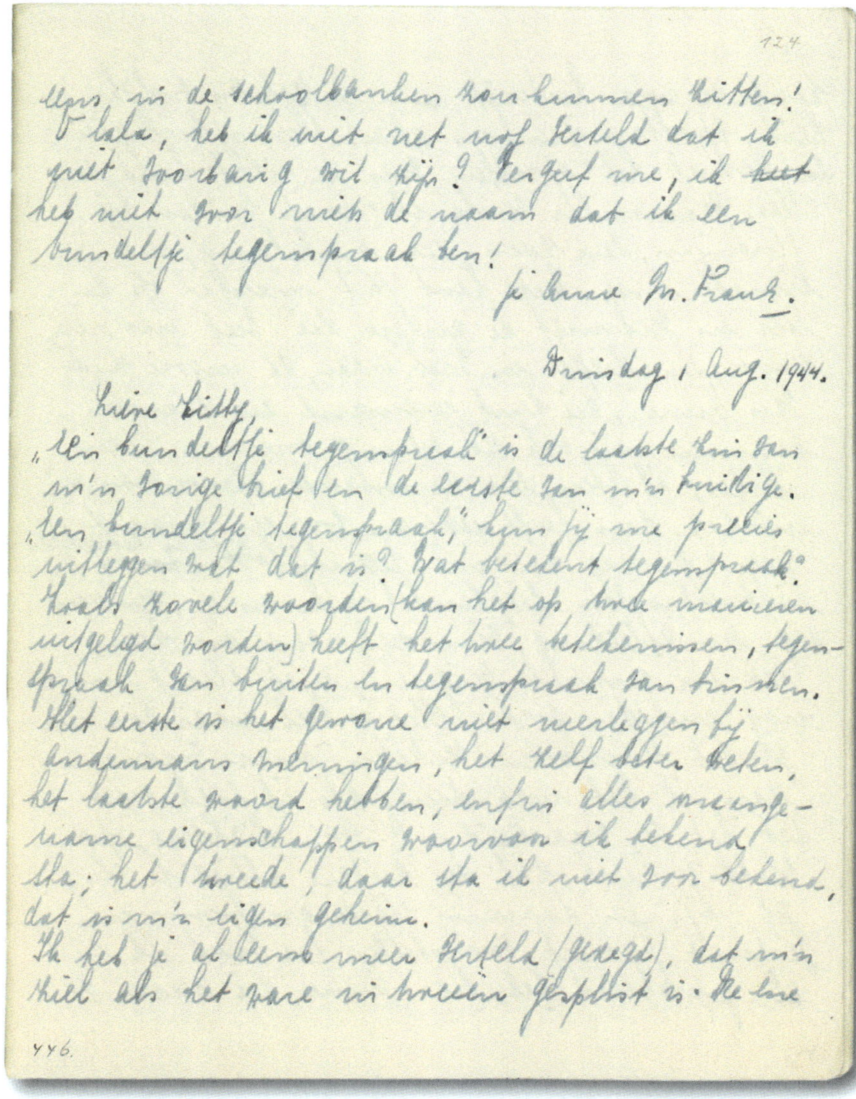
124

ons in de schoolbanken zou kunnen zitten! O lala, heb ik niet net nog verteld dat ik niet voorbarig wil zijn? Vergeef me, ik heet niet voor niets de naam dat ik een bundeltje tegenspraak ben!

je Anne M. Frank.

Dinsdag 1 Aug. 1944.

Lieve Kitty,

„Een bundeltje tegenspraak" is de laatste zin van m'n vorige brief en de eerste van m'n huidige. „Een bundeltje tegenspraak", kun jij me precies uitleggen wat dat is? Wat betekent tegenspraak? Zoals zovele woorden (kan het op twee manieren uitgelegd worden) heeft het twee betekenissen, tegenspraak van buiten en tegenspraak van binnen. Het eerste is het gewone niet neerleggen bij andermans meningen, het zelf beter weten, het laatste woord hebben, enfin alles onaangename eigenschappen waarvoor ik bekend sta; het tweede, daar sta ik niet voor bekend, dat is m'n eigen geheim.
Ik heb je al eens meer verteld (gezegd), dat m'n ziel als het ware in tweeën gesplitst is. De ene

146.

ANNE AT HER DESK in the Amsterdam home to which the Franks moved in 1933, opposite. The last entry of her diary, seen above, was written three days before the Gestapo arrested everyone in the Achterhuis.

wrote, "Oh, Kitty, the best part about the invasion is that I have the feeling that friends are on the way."

But even though freedom seemed near, there was always the fear that someone might betray them: "One small act of carelessness and we're done for!"

In May 1944, the Nazis arrested the greengrocer who had been supplying their vegetables for hiding two Jews. The pressure was debilitating for Anne. Even so, after nearly two years of confinement, she marveled at how she hadn't yet abandoned her hopes: "I cling to them because I still believe, in spite of everything, that people are truly good at heart."

Despite Anne's convictions, neighbors and others had something else in their hearts as they began to sense that there were people hidden at Prinsengracht 263. Bep's younger sister, Nelly, was a Nazi sympathizer and once yelled at Bep, "Go, then, go to your Jews." To rout out every last Jew, the Nazis offered rewards, paying bounty hunters 15 guilders a week as well as an added seven and a half guilders for each Jew discovered.

On August 1, 1944, Anne made what would be her last entry to her friend Kitty. She wrote about how she kept "trying to find a way to become what I'd like to be and what I could be if . . . if only there were no other people in the world."

The world and the people that Anne knew were all about to vanish. She never wrote again. ■

The Franks Are Found

Discovery, Deportation and Death

"These poor people are being shipped off to filthy slaughterhouses like a herd of sick and neglected cattle."

ANNE FRANK, MARCH 27, 1943

POPPERFOTO/GETTY

THE BERGEN-BELSEN concentration camp, where Anne and Margot died in early 1945, shortly before British troops liberated the camp.

It all ended on August 4, 1944, when a tip came in for the security police. The Vienna-born Gestapo *Oberscharführer* Karl Josef Silberbauer, along with members of the Dutch police, arrived at Prinsengracht 263 at around 10:30 that morning. "The door opened and a small man entered," Miep would later recall. "He pointed the revolver in his hand at me and said: 'Stay seated! Don't move!'" They demanded that Victor Kugler tell them who owned this building. As they searched the upstairs, they told him that they knew he had Jews hidden in the building. Feeling he had no other choice, Kugler brought them to the bookcase blocking the Achterhuis and yanked it open.

"When the Gestapo came in with their guns, that was the end of everything," said Otto.

Silberbauer's men searched the apartment, demanding to be led to any money and valuables. When he spotted the leather briefcase containing Anne's writings, he rifled through it but was disappointed to see that there were only some books and loose papers. He then dumped the contents on the floor.

Though Silberbauer seemed to soften when he noticed a trunk marked "Lieutenant of the Reserves Otto Frank" and realized that Otto had fought in World War I, he told the group to get ready to go. He asked how long they had been hiding and didn't believe that it had been two years until Otto pointed to marks on the wall showing how the girls had grown. When they came down to the office, Miep commented on Silberbauer's accent and told him that she too came from Vienna. "Aren't you ashamed of yourself, helping Jewish trash?" he scolded her. "You deserve to receive the worst punishment."

After 25 months of hiding, the Franks, the van Pelses, and Pfeffer were herded out "like beaten dogs," said Miep, and carted away in a truck.

Miep, Jan, Bep, and another employee headed into the Achterhuis. The place had been ransacked. "On the floor, amidst the chaos of papers and books, my eye lit on the little red-orange checked, cloth-bound diary that Anne had received from her father on her 13th birthday," Miep later wrote. She and Bep gathered the papers—there was no sign of Margot's journal—and Miep put them in the bottom drawer of her desk in her office, noting to her colleague that she intended to "keep everything safe for Anne until she comes back."

The next day, Miep headed to the Gestapo office and offered Silberbauer money to gain her friends' release. He said he couldn't help her. Miep then went to see his supervisor but was again unsuccessful. Jo Kleiman and Kugler were meanwhile sent to a prison in town and soon taken to the Amersfoort concentration camp near Utrecht.

The Achterhuis residents—just eight of the 8,000 to 9,000 Dutch Jews that the Nazis discovered

FINE ART IMAGES/HERITAGE IMAGES/GETTY

ALBERT DE JONG/AFP/GETTY

KARL SILBERBAUER, left, the Gestapo sergeant who led the raid on the Achterhuis and dragged the residents away. Above: The aftermath of a June 1943 arrest of several people in eastern Amsterdam.

hiding during the war—were shipped to Westerbork, the transit camp that served as the spot from which the Germans sent Holland's Jews to their deaths at such camps as Auschwitz, Sobibor, Theresienstadt, and Bergen-Belsen. The 97,776 Jews who would pass through Westerbork made up more than 75 percent of the nation's Jewish population.

On September 3, 1944, detainees at Westerbork were roused at dawn. As SS soldiers yelled at them and attack dogs menaced, the Nazis crammed 498 men, 442 women, and 79 children into cattle cars. The train would be the last to leave Holland for Auschwitz, and Anne and the seven others were among 1,019 on board. Limited light filtered into the hot and muggy train, which had only a bucket for a toilet.

At around two in the morning on September 5, the train pulled into Auschwitz in southern Poland. There they were greeted with harsh floodlights, soldiers with machine guns and whips, and the sign over the gate that read ARBEIT MACHT FREI—Work Sets You Free. Those arriving at Auschwitz were either sent to the left

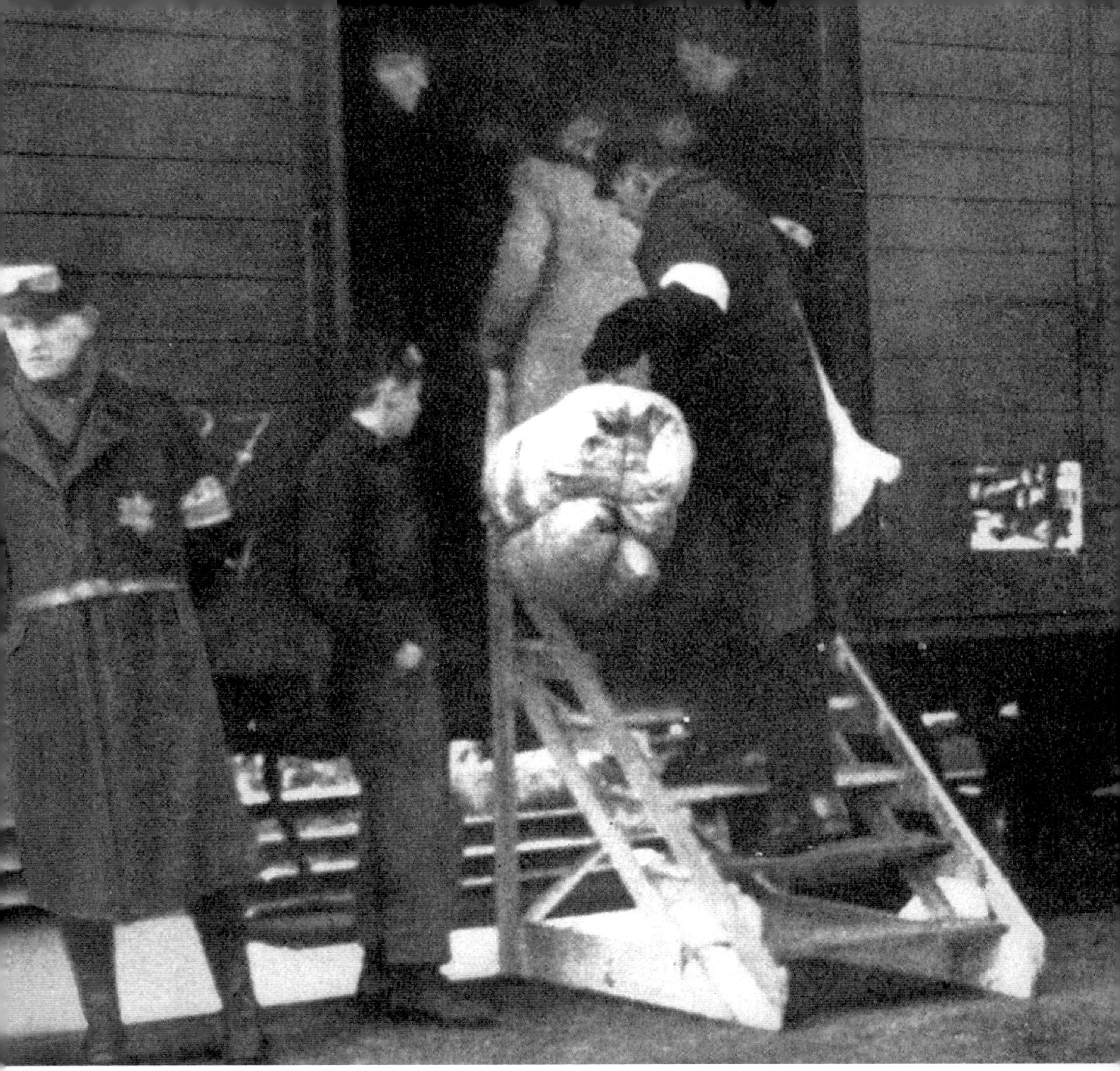

for a quick death or to the right for a slow one from work, starvation, and beating.

"Compared with this, Dante's inferno seems almost a comedy to me," wrote Nazi doctor Johann Kremer, who with the infamous Josef Mengele performed ghastly medical experiments on prisoners. "Auschwitz is not called a death camp for nothing."

Half of those on the Franks' train—549 Jews, including every child under age 15—were directed to the left to gas chambers, where the Nazis asphyxiated them with Zyklon B, a hydrogen cyanide pesticide. Gold fillings were yanked from the teeth of the dead. Their hair was turned into blankets, textiles, ropes, and pipe insulation. Their bodies were sent to crematoriums and their ashes and unburnt bones used as fertilizer or dumped in ponds. Anne's friend Eva Schloss recalls that the air "smelled like burning, singed meat."

All the Achterhuis residents headed to the right, but the men and women walked separately. Otto would never again see Edith, Margot, and Anne.

Auschwitz included three main camps; Otto, Fritz, Hermann, and Peter were sent to Auschwitz I. A few weeks later, Hermann hurt his thumb digging a trench and the next day the Nazis gassed him. "One day in Auschwitz, I was very depressed. I had been beaten the day before," Otto recalled of the unrelenting pressure. "It was a Sunday morning and I said,

FOTOTECA GILARDI/AKG-IMAGES

PRISONERS WERE loaded onto cattle cars with little ventilation for the trip to Westerbork. Lenie van Naarden de Jong, who rode on the train with the Franks, recalled that "many people, also the Frank girls, slept against their mother or father. Everyone was dead tired."

'I can't get up.' And then my comrades... said to me, 'That's not possible, you must get up, otherwise you are lost.'" With the help of a Dutch doctor, Otto was moved to the sick barracks.

Meanwhile, Anne, Margot, Edith, and Auguste had their heads shaved and were showered, covered with delousing powder, and tattooed, with Anne, Margot, and Edith assigned numbers falling between A-25060 and A-25271. They were sent to Women's Block 29 in Auschwitz II, where they worked 12 hours a day as slave laborers and slept in crowded bunks. Throughout, all the prisoners were subjected to punishment by SS guards like Irma Grese, known as the Hyena of Auschwitz, who took pleasure in stomping people with her jackboots. The tension in the camp was horrendous. "There were people who threw themselves against the electric fence," recalled survivor Lenie van Naarden de Jong. In this environment, any animosity between Anne and her mother vanished. "In the camp, all of that actually completely fell away," recalled Margot's classmate Bloeme Evers-Emden, who arrived on their train from Westerbork. "By giving each other mutual support, they were able to keep each other alive."

They subsisted on scarce rations of thin soup and bread. Edith exchanged her shoes for extra food for her daughters—food that she never received. Soon the girls developed scabies. "The Frank girls looked terrible, their hands and bodies covered with spots and sores from the scabies," said fellow inmate Ronnie Goldstein–van Cleef. "They were in a very bad way; pitiful." Because of their sickness, Anne and Margot were sent to a barracks without their mother. Van Naarden de Jong then helped Edith dig a hole to pass bread to the girls.

The Germans were losing the war and the Russians were approaching, so the Nazis started moving prisoners to other locations to work in factories. In October 1944, the Germans transported Fritz to the Neuengamme concentration camp. He died there on December 20, 1944. They sent Peter, via death march, to Mauthausen in January 1945, and he died in May, at the time of the camp's liberation.

Though the Frank women were left in Auschwitz during one selection of prisoners to send to another camp—likely because Anne was sick—there was another round of selections in October 1944. A thousand women were forced to stand naked on the parade ground as a camp doctor inspected them. "Then it was the turn of both girls... and there they stood for that moment, naked and bald," recalled another prisoner, Rosa de Winter-Levy, of how the doctor chose Anne and Margot but not Edith. "Anne looked straight at us with her innocent eyes, and then they were gone. We weren't able to see what happened to them next. We heard Mrs. Frank cry out: 'The children! Oh God...'"

That was the last time the girls saw their mother, who would die on January 6, 1945, three weeks before the Russians liberated Auschwitz.

The Nazis crammed Anne and Margot and 1,306 others into a train for a trip of several days to Bergen-Belsen in northern Germany. Auguste might have been on that transport, too. After they arrived, the sisters met up with Amsterdammers Jannie Brandes-Brilleslijper and her sister, Lientje, whom they had met in Westerbork.

"Rudolph Höss would quite likely have wound up as some sort of drab functionary . . . Instead, he evolved, step by step, into one of the greatest criminals in history."

AUSCHWITZ PRISONER AND AUTHOR PRIMO LEVI ON THE CAMP'S COMMANDANT

UNIVERSAL HISTORY ARCHIVE/GETTY

YAD VASHEM PHOTO ARCHIVES/AP

"We saw two thin, bald figures that looked like freezing baby birds," said Lientje. "We fell into each other's arms and cried."

Guards placed the women in a massive tent camp, and the four of them "cuddled up with each other under our blankets. The first few days were peaceful, we slept a lot," Lientje recalled. "Then it started to rain." A few days after they arrived, a violent storm knocked over their tent, and they had to cower in a barn. "Why do they want us to live like animals?" Anne asked Jannie, who answered, "Because they are man-eating wild animals themselves."

Soon Anne and Margot were transferred to a barracks. Anne and Margot slept in a lower bunk beside the door, where they were assaulted by the wind. One of the other prisoners, Rachel van Amerongen-Frankfoorder, would later recall that it was possible to "see both of them dying."

In December, the women got a small piece of cheese and some jam. "We wanted to celebrate St. Nicholas Day, Hanukkah, and Christmas in our own way," said Lientje. From

some Hungarian girls who worked in the kitchen they received potato peels. "Anne managed to get hold of a stick of celery," Lientje recalled. "The Daniel sisters found some red beets. I sang and danced for some guards and got a handful of sauerkraut. We had saved our bread, and with all this together we made a surprise present for the others. We roasted the potato peels and quietly sang Dutch and Yiddish songs, and imagined what we would do if we ever got home. Anne's idea was: 'Then we'll have a party, a celebratory meal at Dikker & Thijs,' one of Amsterdam's most expensive restaurants. For a little while we were almost happy."

This respite was, of course, fleeting. Both girls were sick—Margot

CONTINUED ON PAGE 71

DR. JOSEF MENGELE, far left in photo opposite, became known as the Angel of Death for experiments he performed on prisoners. To his left are Auschwitz commandant Rudolf Höss, Josef Kramer, who would soon run Bergen-Belsen, and an unidentified officer. Jews from Czechoslovakia, above, being sorted at Auschwitz. Some went straight to gas chambers; others were worked to death.

HUGO JAEGER/THE PICTURE COLLECTION, INC.

AMID TULIPS and to the strains of a Viennese waltz, Adolf Hitler, left, chats with future Reichskommissar of the Netherlands Arthur Seyss-Inquart, Margarete Himmler, and her husband, Reichsführer-SS Heinrich Himmler, the second most powerful man in Nazi Germany, in Munich in February 1939, just before their invasion of Poland.

POPPERFOTO/GETTY

CONTINUED FROM PAGE 67

with diarrhea—and stayed behind when their friends were transferred to a different barracks. Anne's classmate Nanette Blitz Konig recalled that Anne "was no more than a skeleton by then." Konig, who had attended the party at which Anne received her diary, said that despite her state, Anne spoke of the future, mentioning how she hoped to use her journal to write about what happened.

Lice plagued the prisoners, and Jannie said that "at a certain moment in her final days, Anne stood in front of me, wrapped in a blanket. She didn't have any more tears, and she told me that she had such a horror of the lice and fleas in her clothes and that she had thrown all of her clothes away. It was the middle of winter and she was wrapped in one blanket."

Anne's friend Hannah Pick-Goslar and her family had been placed in a section of the camp for inmates whom the Nazis considered valuable and hoped to exchange for German prisoners. Conditions there were not as harsh, and they had more food. In early 1945, Hannah heard that some other Dutch women had arrived. "They were very, very near to us. The Germans didn't allow us to speak to them. They put up a high fence and they put straw in it so we couldn't even see the women, but we heard them," she tells LIFE. "Somehow we learned that there were 40 women from Holland. One day somebody told me, 'You know, your friend Anne is here next to us.' Then at night I went in the dark as far as I could near this fence I called, 'Hello. Hello.' One of the Dutch women answered me. It was Mrs. van Pels. She said, 'Oh, you want Anne?' I waited in the cold and rainy night, but not too long, and then a very sad and weak voice is calling for me and it was Anne. At the beginning we both cried."

The friends spoke of their families, and Anne "asked if I could help with some food." Hannah's section had received small packages from the Red Cross, and she told Anne to come back in two days and she would see what she could do. Hannah collected some bread, prunes, socks, and gloves. "After two or three days I came with this little football. I threw it over. But it was night and it was dark and the fence was high. One of the other hungry women caught the package and ran away with it. Anne was angry and crying and awfully, very, very sad. I promised I would do it again, and this time she caught the package."

Soon after that, Hannah's father, Hans, died. She didn't return to the fence for several days. By then, the Germans had moved Anne's group, and Hannah never talked with her again. The Nazis sent Auguste van Pels to Raguhn, a subcamp at Buchenwald. Two months later they shipped her to Theresienstadt, and she soon died.

After Anne and Margot arrived at Bergen-Belsen, a man named Josef Kramer took over as commandant. "The more dead Jews you bring me, the better I like it," he said, and he quickly earned the nickname the Beast of Belsen. As the Russian army neared, Kramer added torture, beating, and machine-gunning of inmates in burial trenches to the hell that already existed in the camp. And with overcrowding, rations were cut even further. Typhus, diphtheria, tuberculosis, and dysentery coursed through the camp's population. Five hundred

USING SHOES of the dead as fuel, women cooked over open fires soon after the liberation of Bergen-Belsen concentration camp. Allied medical officers there wiped out the typhus that had killed Anne and Margot.

GEORGE RODGER/LIFE/THE PICTURE COLLECTION

people died each day. Corpses littered the ground.

Anne and Margot contracted typhus, which brought on muscle pain, headaches, fever, rashes, and delirium. Jannie and Lientje found the sisters in the sick barracks and warned them not to stay there. But Anne said, "Here we can both lie on one bunk, we are together, and it's peaceful."

Jannie and Lientje visited the next day. "Margot had fallen out of the bunk and was barely conscious," Lientje recalled. "Anne had a fever too; she was friendly and sweet. She said, 'Margot will sleep well and when she sleeps I won't need to get up again.'"

When Jannie and Lientje returned a few days later they found Anne and Margot's bunk empty.

"We knew what that meant," Lientje said. "We found them behind the barrack, wrapped their thin bodies in a blanket, and carried them to a mass grave. That was all we could do for them." ■

BRITISH SOLDIERS watch as female Nazi camp guards place bodies in a mass grave at Bergen-Belsen, above. The quick burials were necessary to stop the spread of typhus. In March 1957, a German woman and her daughter, opposite, set flowers at a mass grave at Bergen-Belsen during "Brotherhood Week," which was started by the Society for Christian-Jewish Co-Operation in Hamburg. Anne and Margot are two of the 30,000 buried at the camp.

BETTMANN/GETTY

HERE LIE BURIE
1000 BODIES
HIER RUHEN
1000 TOTE
24.4.45

Her Voice Lives On

The Publication of Anne's Diary

"It's utterly impossible for me to build my life on a foundation of chaos, suffering, and death."

ANNE FRANK, JULY 15, 1944

ARNOLD NEWMAN/GETTY

OTTO FRANK at the Achterhuis on the morning of its opening as a museum, in May 1960.

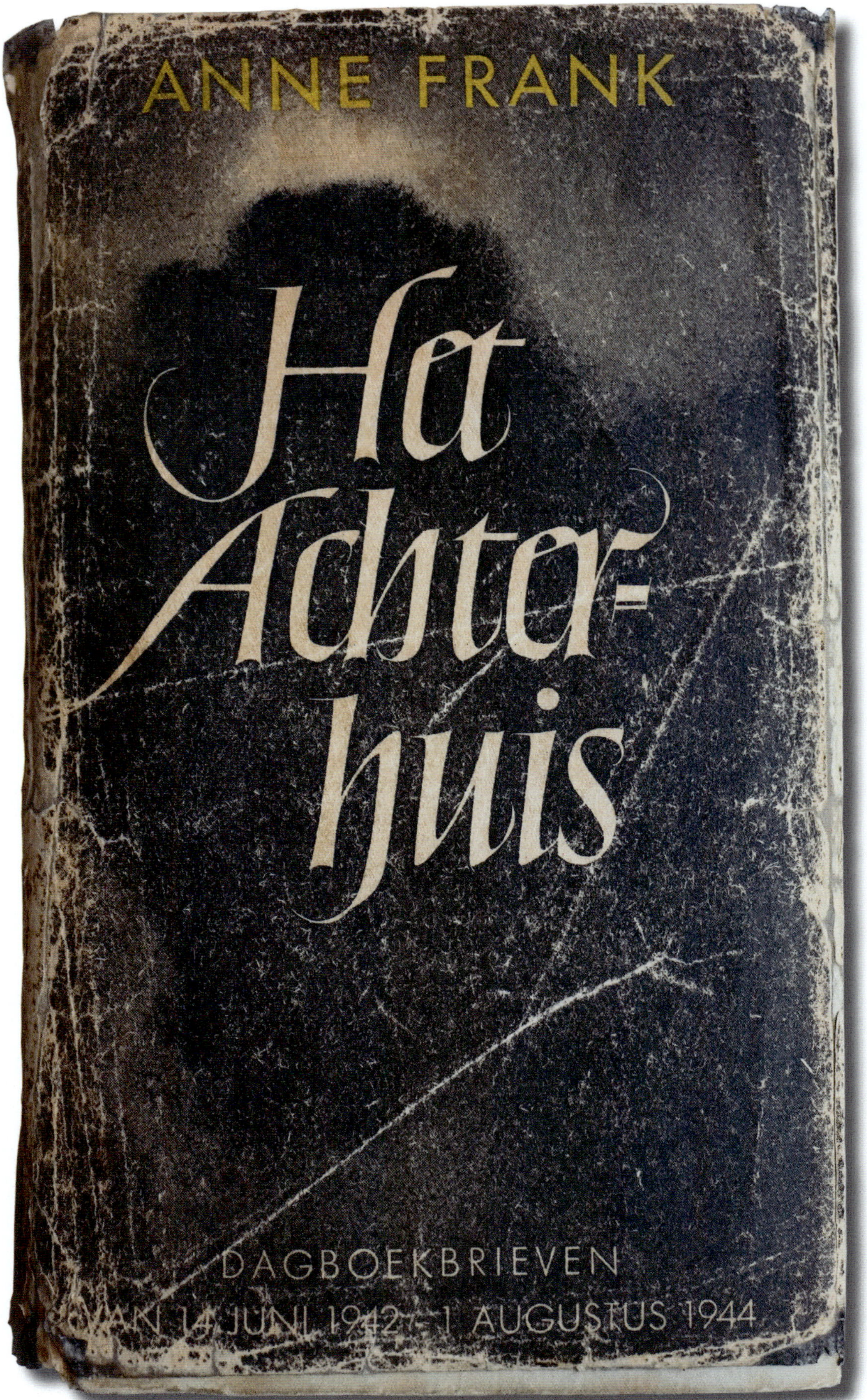

TON KOENE/HORIZONS/AKG-IMAGES

During the years of the Holocaust, the Nazis systematically murdered six million Jews, as well as five million Roma, Sinti, priests, nuns, people with disabilities, homosexuals, and political prisoners. The killing took place throughout Europe in more than 40,000 concentration, labor, prisoner of war, and internment camps, as well as by the *Einsatzgruppen,* mobile killing squads, which machine-gunned entire communities or shoved residents into gas-asphyxiation vans.

Some 80 percent of Dutch Jews died in the Holocaust, giving Holland the highest death rate in western Europe. Of the 107,000 Dutch Jews sent to the camps, only 5,000 lived. The death toll at Auschwitz, where more than a million people died, proved especially high. Of the 60,000 Dutch Jews shipped to Auschwitz, just 673 survived, including 127 men and women who had been on the Frank family's transport there in September of 1944.

Otto Frank was one of them, having been spared because he had been placed in the sick barracks before the Russian army liberated the camp on January 27, 1945.

When the nearly six foot tall Otto left Poland, he weighed less than 115 pounds. He knew that Edith had died, but he was determined to make his way back to Amsterdam. "All my hope is the children," he wrote to his mother in Switzerland. "I cling to the conviction that they are alive and that we will be together again."

Miep Gies and Bep Voskuijl had kept the firm going during the war. Jo

ANNE'S DIARY, published as *Het Achterhuis* (*The Secret Annex*), opposite, appeared in June 1947. Below: Jan and Miep Gies—with Otto, at back—play with their son, Paul, who was born in July 1950. When Paul arrived, Miep stopped working at Opekta.

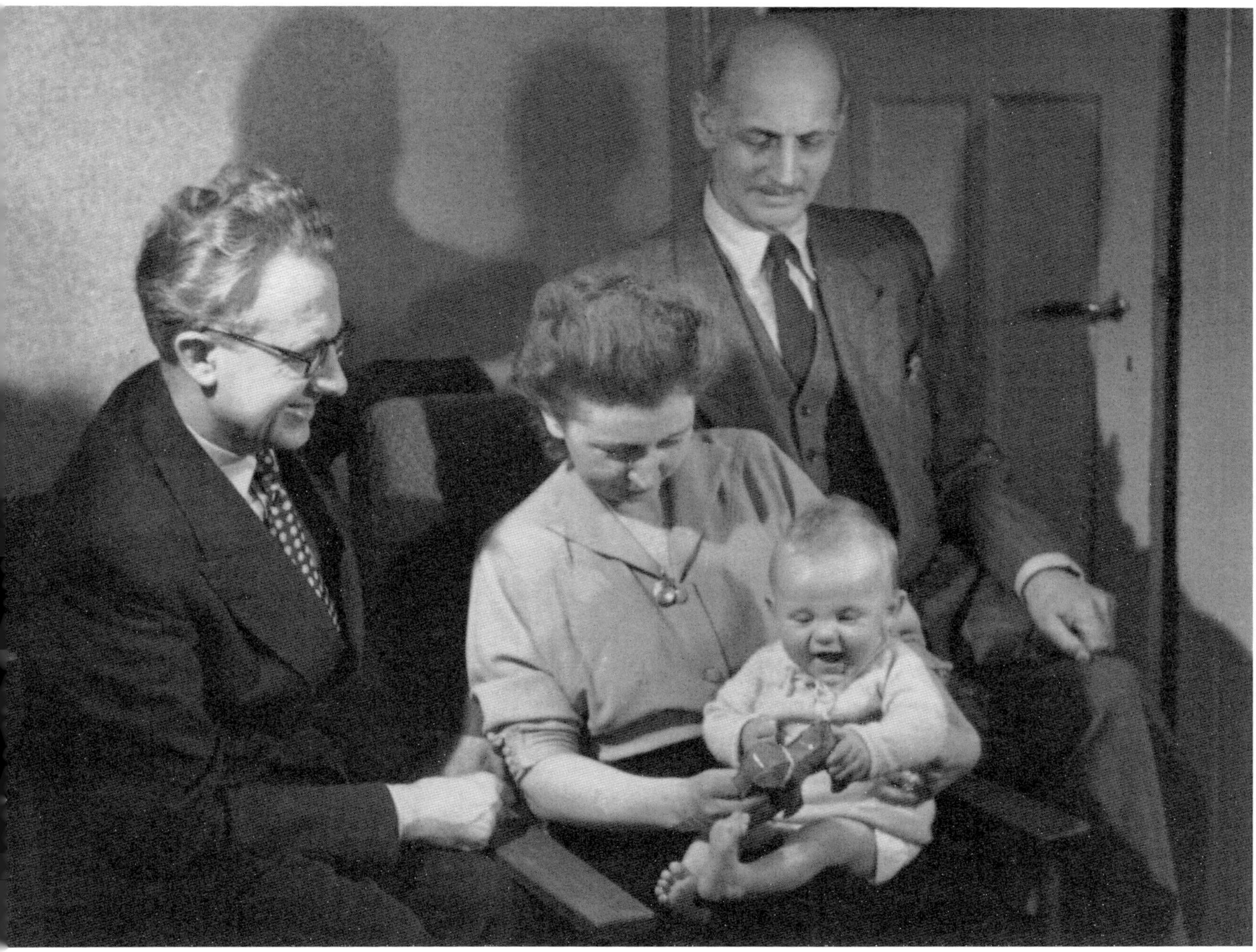

Kleiman, who was released from the Amerfoort concentration camp soon after his arrest because of his health, made it back to the firm too. Yet, as the war drew to an end and the Allies advanced, conditions throughout the Netherlands continued to deteriorate. Distribution of food and supplies was disrupted, and citizens chopped down trees and dismantled homes for fuel. Some resorted to eating tulip bulbs, and more than 20,000 Netherlanders starved to death during what became known as the Hunger Winter. "All conversations centered on food," wrote Miep. "Food obsessions were affecting all our minds." After Canadian troops liberated Amsterdam in May 1945, displaced residents staggered home. Victor Kugler, who escaped from the Nazis during a forced march, returned to work.

Then on June 3, Otto Frank rang Miep and Jan Gies's doorbell.

Miep would later recall how, after standing speechless for a time, Otto released the "thunderbolt" of news that Edith would not return but that he held out hope for his daughters.

Otto moved in with the Gieses, went back to Opekta, and put ads in papers seeking information on Anne and Margot. Finally, in July, he heard that Jannie Brandes-Brilleslijper might know of their fate. On the 18th of that month, he went to her home.

"I could hardly speak because it was very difficult to tell someone that his children were not alive anymore," Jannie recalled. "I said, 'They are no more.' He turned deathly pale and slumped down into a chair."

After the Red Cross confirmed their deaths, and Miep knew that Anne would not be coming back for the diary, she told Otto that she had kept it and 327 loose papers safe. Though he was at first too overwhelmed to read the testament his daughter had left of her short life, eventually he girded himself to learn what Anne had written. What he found, he would recall, was "so unbelievably exciting" that he could barely put it down.

Not only the diary but also the revisions that Anne had made as she dreamed of creating a novel and launching her career had miraculously survived. "This brilliant young girl revised her diary because she discovered that she had become a much better writer," the novelist Philip Roth, who conjured up Anne in his novels *The Ghost Writer, Exit Ghost,* and *My Life as a Man,* has observed. "The fact that she rewrote it is one sign that, had she survived, she would have achieved an important literary career."

Otto reunited with old friends. Eva Schloss and her mother, Elfriede, survived Auschwitz. One day Otto came by with a small parcel under his arm and carefully took out Anne's diary. "It was very emotional," Schloss tells

RALPH CRANE/LIFE/THE PICTURE COLLECTION (2)

THE DIARY OF ANNE FRANK **opened on Broadway in October 1955 and ran for 717 performances, receiving a Pulitzer Prize and a Tony Award. Above, left: A scene from the movie version of the diary. Above: A set from the film, which opened in April 1959 and won three Oscars.**

LIFE. "He read a few sentences but he always broke into tears."

He had decided that it would be his mission to share Anne's words with the world. Otto had the diary typed up, though he shifted a few entries and omitted sections that were critical of her mother and of Fritz Pfeffer, as well as certain entries that included Anne's musings on her emerging sexuality.

It proved difficult to find a publisher until one of Otto's friends showed it to the historian Jan Romein, who wrote a front-page article with the headline *"Kinderstem"* ("A Child's Voice") for the April 3, 1946, edition of the newspaper *Het Parool.* "To me, however, this apparently inconsequential diary by a child," Romein wrote, "stammered out in a child's voice, embodies all the hideousness of fascism, more so than all the evidence at Nuremberg put together." Soon after, the Amsterdam publisher Contact agreed to publish the book, and on June 25, 1947, it appeared as *Het Achterhuis* (*The Secret*

"I was exactly the right age to be on my own. If I had been younger, like my sister, I would have stayed with my parents. If I were older, with children, I just don't know how I could have done it."

BARBARA LEDERMANN RODBELL, ON HER DECISION TO WORK WITH THE RESISTANCE

PAUL SCHUTZER/LIFE/THE PICTURE COLLECTION

ANNE AND HER FRIEND Susanne "Sanne" Ledermann playing in Amsterdam, left. Sanne died in Auschwitz in 1943. Her sister, Barbara, was able to pass as a non-Jew. "I changed my name, I took off my star, I became a non-Jewish person," she said. Barbara worked with the underground to save other Jews. After the war, she emigrated to the United States. She is seen above attending a showing of the Academy Award–winning film with her husband, Martin Rodbell, who would win the 1994 Nobel Prize in Physiology or Medicine.

ANNE FRANK FONDS, BASEL/GETTY

Annex). Otto gave copies to family, friends, the Dutch prime minister, and the royal family. (Miep Gies could not bring herself to read it until the second edition appeared.)

Only two years had passed since the end of the war, but for many the book by the 15-year-old who had written that she still believed that "people are truly good at heart" already proved useful as a way to personalize the Holocaust. "Not only do you have a name and a face and a person in the case of Anne Frank, but you have a very well written diary. It is captivating," Professor Deborah Lipstadt, author of *Denying the Holocaust,* tells LIFE. "She is a good writer and she knows how to express herself. She is expressing herself in something she doesn't even know will see the light of day."

Meanwhile, with the war's end the Allies scrambled to round up the Nazi leadership and punish those responsible for the deaths of millions. Reichskommissar Arthur Seyss-Inquart, who led the assault on Holland, was executed following the Nuremberg trials. Auschwitz

ANNE FRANK FONDS, BASEL/GETTY (2)

commandant Rudolph Höss was tried in Warsaw and hanged at the camp he had run. Bergen-Belsen's Josef Kramer and Irma Grese were hanged as well. The Dutch tried Hanns Rauter, who had overseen security during the occupation of Amsterdam, and executed him in 1949.

And Karl Josef Silberbauer, the man who arrested the Achterhuis residents, served 14 months in prison for mistreatment of communists. In 1954 he joined the Vienna police. It was there, in 1963, that Nazi hunter Simon Wiesenthal discovered him. When Wiesenthal revealed to the world that Silberbauer had been the one to arrest Anne, the force suspended him, causing Silberbauer to complain that he needed his paycheck to pay off some furniture he had just purchased on installment. Otto, though, said that Silberbauer had only been following orders in August 1944 and that no one had been ill-treated during the raid that led to the slaughter of his family and the others. His comments helped bring about Silberbauer's reinstatement to the police force.

Otto began to spend more time with Eva Schloss and her mother, Elfriede. "I was very depressed, I was very miserable," says Eva. "I was the same age as his daughter. Gradually, as he realized that I needed help, he helped me. He liked to help people. I was sort of a surrogate." By the early 1950s, Otto had settled in Basel, Switzerland, and in 1953 he married Elfriede. It was a relationship that

OTTO AND ELFRIEDE, his second wife, above, visit the Anne Frank Memorial Forest in Israel in the mid 1960s. Opposite, top: Hannah Pick-Goslar, far left next to Anne, was one of Anne's closest friends. Anne dreamed of her while in the Achterhuis, and Hannah was one of the last people to speak with Anne at Bergen-Belsen before her death. Hannah's mother and father died during the war, and after the war Otto helped her move to Switzerland. Soon after, she settled in Israel and raised her family, bottom.

PAUL SCHUTZER/LIFE/THE PICTURE COLLECTION

RO*CO FILMS INTERNATIONAL/EVERETT

MARGOT AND OTTO VISITED her cousin Bernhard "Buddy" Elias in Switzerland in the 1930s, opposite. Elias's family moved there before Hitler's rise to power. In 1996, Elias became president of the Anne Frank Fonds, a foundation that protects Anne's legacy. He visited a memorial to her and Margot in Bergen-Belsen in 2015, above, just before his own death.

ANNE FRANK FONDS, BASEL/GETTY

Eva originally struggled with. "I was always introduced as Anne Frank's stepsister," says Eva, who has written a number of books about her own experiences, including *Eva's Story: A Survivor's Tale by the Stepsister of Anne Frank*. "At first it annoyed me. Eventually I got over that."

It was the 1952 publication of the American edition of the diary that catapulted Anne's book to international acclaim, helped by an introduction by former First Lady Eleanor Roosevelt, who called it "one of the wisest and most moving commentaries on war and its impact on human beings that I have ever read." A theatrical adaptation opened on Broadway in 1955 with Susan Strasberg as Anne; it won both the Tony Award for Best Play and the Pulitzer Prize for Drama. A film version appeared four years later and earned three Academy Awards. (The play has been performed internationally over the years in both professional and amateur productions, including a 1997 Tony-nominated revival in which 16-year-old Natalie Portman made her Broadway debut as Anne.)

The words of this most famous victim of the Holocaust have been translated into 70 languages, and more than 30 million copies of the diary have been sold.

Yet from the start, the book had its detractors. Some called it a forgery, saying that even a precocious 15-year-old could not have written it. Others denied that Anne ever existed. "These people are Holocaust deniers, they are conspiracy theorists, they are people

AT THE ANNE FRANK School in Düsseldorf, on the occasion of the opening of the sixth Anne Frank Village for refugees, Otto talked with a new generation of German schoolchildren about his daughter's legacy, in July 1969.

AP

"Young people especially always want to know how these terrible things could have happened. I answer them as well as I can."

OTTO FRANK

who believe in lies," says Lipstadt. "At the heart it is an anti-Semitism that makes them believe that Jews have made all this up."

Otto fought each attack on his daughter's legacy. German handwriting experts studied the manuscripts and concluded that the work was by Anne. A further blow to the deniers' claims appeared when Wiesenthal discovered Silberbauer, who admitted that he had arrested Anne Frank.

To protect Anne's memory, Otto in 1963 founded the Anne Frank Fonds, a charitable foundation, in Basel. When he died in August 1980, he willed his estate and copyright ownership of the diary to the foundation. "Our main priority is to protect the diary and our duty is to make sure that the diary is available in a full version," board member Yves Kugelmann tells LIFE. As part of its mission, the foundation ensures that Anne's work reaches as many people as possible and a few years ago translated it into Arabic, Farsi, and Turkish. "We use it for education to explain why the Holocaust can't be denied." Since Otto opposed the commercialization of his daughter's work, income from the diary supports charitable and educational programs, such as the Israeli village of Neve Shalom/Wahat al-Salam—where Jews, Palestinians, Muslims, and Christians live together peacefully—and an orphanage in Kathmandu, Nepal.

The actual diary and papers went to the Dutch state, with stewardship of the manuscripts entrusted to the NIOD Institute for War, Holocaust, and Genocide Studies. To end any further controversy surrounding her work, in the early 1980s the institute began an exhaustive study of the writings. "There had been some 50 attacks on the authenticity of the diary by right-wingers and Holocaust deniers," David Barnouw, who coedited a critical edition for the institute, tells LIFE. "There are still people who also believe the earth is flat. So we did an investigation into the paper and the ink and the glue that was used in the diary." The study confirmed that only Anne penned the entries.

On June 12, 1989, on what would have been Anne's 60th birthday, the institute brought out their critical edition, containing Anne's original diary, her own revisions, and the published version. Then in 1998, five unknown pages written by Anne were discovered. These contained items that Otto had purposely left out, such as passages Anne had written that were critical of her mother. These pages were included in a 2001 edition.

And in 2015, the Anne Frank Fonds named Otto and one of the other editors who helped prepare the manuscript as its official coauthors so that the European copyright on the diary would endure until 2050. (The American copyright expires in the 2040s.) The foundation is now working with Cambridge University Press to publish a new critical edition. And, in an effort to reach a new generation of readers who approach books differently, they are also creating a graphic diary. "We have to make this balance between our wish to keep everything very authentic but also to understand the language of young people of today," says Kugelmann. "You have to find a way to tell the story." ■

EXIT

MARTYN HAYHOW/AFP/GETTY

Securing the Memory

The House and the Legacy

"I don't want to have lived in vain like most people. I want to be useful or bring enjoyment to all people, even those I've never met. I want to go on living even after my death!"

ANNE FRANK, APRIL 5, 1944

IN MEMORIAM Anne Frank, **a choral work by Howard Goodall written to commemorate the 50th anniversary of her death, was performed by the Voices Foundation Children's Choir at Westminster Central Hall in London on January 27, 2001.**

To many, the millions of people killed by the Nazis represent an unfathomable number, a statistic bled of humanity. While Anne Frank was just one of those lost in that vast sea of death, through her writings from the 25 months in hiding she gave a voice to those who perished. "Anne," says her friend Eva Schloss, "became the representation of the 1.5 million children who were murdered."

Otto Frank had long worried about how the world would remember his daughter. He didn't want her to become a mythical figure, says Yves Kugelmann of the Anne Frank Fonds, but rather hoped that his daughter would be remembered as a writer, for the striking book she produced.

And she has—but the ways in which her life has made an impact have also stretched far beyond the pages of the diary.

President John F. Kennedy commented in 1961 that "no voice is more compelling than that of Anne Frank." She has been invoked by world leaders from South Africa's Nelson Mandela to Czechoslovakia's Vaclav Havel. The Italian novelist and Auschwitz survivor Primo Levi wrote, "One single Anne Frank moves us more than the countless others who suffered just as she did but whose faces have remained in the shadows."

When Otto Frank returned to Amsterdam, Prinsengracht 263 was in a dilapidated state. In the 1950s a textile firm sought to buy up buildings in the area to construct a factory. By then, Anne's diary had already become a best-seller, and in 1957 a committee of scientists and intellectuals struck a deal to preserve the site on Prinsengracht. The buildings were renovated and opened to the public as a museum, the Anne Frank House, in May 1960.

The building on Prinsengracht continues to bear witness to Anne's all-too-brief presence on earth. Each year, about a million visitors pass behind the hinged bookcase and climb the stairs to the cramped hideout where a writer once began to bloom. And near Westerkerk church, whose ringing bells Anne found so reassuring, stands a statue of Anne.

Jo Kleiman died in 1959, Victor Kugler in 1981, Bep Voskuijl in 1983. Throughout, Miep Gies humbly shouldered the burden of unsought fame, always reiterating that thousands of other righteous Dutch people had also helped those in need during the Nazi occupation. Miep and Jan spent each August 4, the day of the raid, sitting quietly at their Amsterdam home with the curtains drawn and the phone turned off.

MIQUEL GONZALEZ/LAIF/REDUX

"Every day of my life, I've wished that things had been different," she wrote. "That even had Anne's diary been lost to the world, Anne and the others might somehow have been saved. Not a day goes by that I do not grieve for them." When Miep traveled and talked with schoolchildren and others about Anne and the Holocaust, she wore her own memento of the Achterhuis—a diamond and black onyx ring that Auguste van Pels gave her.

In the mid 1980s, Miep collaborated with Alison Leslie Gold on the book *Anne Frank Remembered* and helped Jon Blair make an Academy Award–winning documentary of the same name in 1995. Jan Gies died in 1993, and two years later

A CANAL BOAT placidly cruises past the Anne Frank House museum, which welcomes about a million visitors each year. Prinsengracht 263 is at left, with the green-painted ground floor.

"So much had been lost, but now Anne's voice would never be lost. My young friend had left a remarkable legacy to the world."

MIEP GIES

Queen Beatrix knighted Miep in the Order of Orange-Nassau. Then in 2010, Miep, the most dogged of the Achterhuis helpers, died at age 100. That August, the old chestnut tree "on whose branches little raindrops shine, appearing like silver," as Anne once noted, collapsed from disease. Before the ailing tree fell, scores of cuttings were taken from it and distributed around the world to grow new trees. One was placed at the U.S. Capitol; Bill Clinton planted another at his presidential library in Little Rock, Arkansas.

And, all these years later, Anne Frank's legacy continues to grow too.

Her cousin Bernhard "Buddy" Elias served as president of the Anne Frank foundation from 1996 until his death in 2015. He and his wife, Gertrude, lived in a home that he had inherited from his mother, Otto's sister, Helene. In 2001, while cleaning the attic, Gertrude uncovered a trove of some 6,000 letters, postcards, poems, drawings, and photos sent to the Elias family by the Franks before they went into hiding. Anne had enjoyed skating with Buddy—he would go on to become a professional skater—and in one of the letters from 1941 she wrote, "Maybe we can skate as a pair together someday, but I know I'll have to train very hard to be as good as you are."

Elias was also instrumental in turning the Frank family's apartment in Merwedeplein into a writer's residence for those who faced persecution or censorship in their home country. He worked with local groups to renovate the space to reflect what it looked like in the 1930s when the Franks lived there.

And in 2012, Elias oversaw the establishment of the Frank Family Centre. The center, under the auspices of the Anne Frank Fonds, seeks to place Anne's life in the context of centuries of German-Jewish history.

© ANNE FRANK HOUSE, PHOTOGRAPHER ALLARD BOVENBERG

L.E. BASKOW/ZUMA

SPAARNESTAD/HOLLANDSE HOOGTE/REDUX

A DISPLAY at the Anne Frank House recreates what Anne's bedroom in the Secret Annex looked like, at left, above. Lower left: One of the 569,355 yellow stars that the Nazis forced Jews to wear. Jan and Miep Gies stand at the entrance to the Achterhuis, above. "I am not a hero," Miep wrote. "I stand at the end of the long, long line of good Dutch people who did what I did or more."

Anne Franks dagbok
増補新訂版
A・フランク
文春文庫
ANNA FRANK
Diari
dzienni
(Oficyna)
12 czerwca 1942 – 1 sierpnia 1944
Zestawione przez Otto Franka i Mirjam Pressler
znak
Dr. Khalil Wedad
안네 프랑크 지음 / 홍경호 옮김
문학사상사
ANNE FRANKS DAGBOG
Taglibro de
Anne Frank
Tradukis Nora Bartels
Dyddiadur ANNE FRANK
100
ЗАДНАТА КЪЩА
POPULIBROS LA PRENSA
Anne Franki päevik

Set in the family's hometown of Frankfurt and scheduled to open in 2018, it combines various archives and collections and contains photos, paintings, furniture, and memorabilia to help explain the larger meaning of the world in which Anne and her family once lived.

Scholars continue to uncover new details about Anne's life. For example, in December 2016, the Anne Frank House released a study that said it was possible that the Gestapo might have simply stumbled on the Achterhuis by chance while investigating a report of false ration coupons and illegal laborers, rather than having been tipped off about people in hiding. And at the same time many others have seen new relevance in her legacy, especially in light of an ongoing international migrant crisis. Prior to the U.S. presidential election in 2016, Eva Schloss—who cofounded the Anne Frank Trust UK—wrote in a magazine piece that "we haven't really learnt anything" from history if people continue to turn their backs on refugees.

Some lessons, though, will be remembered. In late 2016, architect Daniel Libeskind unveiled a design for a Dutch Holocaust memorial to be set in Amsterdam's historic Jewish quarter. The memorial will be made from the same red bricks for which Amsterdam is renowned, and shaped to spell out *lizkor,* the Hebrew word for "in memory of." Its walls will contain the names and dates of birth and death of the more than 100,000 Jewish, Roma, and Sinti residents of the Netherlands who were killed by the Nazis.

When completed, the memorial will stand as one more reminder of the families, friends, neighbors, and strangers who perished during the Holocaust. And, as with one young girl's diary, it will serve as a warning and lesson for future generations. ■

EDITIONS IN SOME of the 70 languages into which Anne's diary has been translated, opposite. Below: An Israeli child of Dutch parentage climbs on a sculpture at a memorial to Anne Frank in Jerusalem. The steel memorial contains a cutout of the chestnut tree that stood outside the Achterhuis.

HEILKE HELLER/ULLSTEIN BILD/GRANGER
JIM HOLLANDER/EPA/REDUX

HERMAN WOUTERS/THE NEW YORK TIMES/REDUX

THE CHESTNUT TREE that Anne loved to gaze at through the attic window. Before the tree collapsed in 2010, cuttings were taken to plant around the world.

Printed in Great Britain
by Amazon

58113920R00054